Ankur Wai creator whose deep, witty and brutally honest thoughts on success and failure, money and investing, self-awareness and personal relationships have made him one of India's top personal brands.

In his first book, Ankur puts together the key ideas that have fuelled his journey – one that began with him wanting to be a space engineer and ended with him creating content that has been seen and read by millions.

His thoughts range from the importance of creating habits for long-term success to the foundations of money management, from embracing and accepting failure to the real truth about learning empathy.

This is a book to be read, and reread, a book whose lines you will underline and think about again and again, a book you will give your family and friends and strangers. Ankur hopes for this book to become the most gifted book ever!

DO
EPIC
SHIT

ANKUR WARIKOO

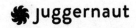 juggernaut

JUGGERNAUT BOOKS
C-I-128, First Floor, Sangam Vihar,
Near Holi Chowk, New Delhi 110080, India

First published in hardback by Juggernaut Books 2021
Published in paperback 2022

10 9 8 7 6 5 4 3 2 1

P-ISBN: 9789393986283
E-ISBN: 9789391165499

Typeset in League Spartan by
R. Ajith Kumar, Noida

Printed at Thomson Press India Ltd

*Dedicated to all the failures and roadblocks I
faced in life. We rarely wish for them,
but upon reflection I realize they are the
reason I am here today.*

CONTENTS

Contents

INTRODUCTION

This book may very well turn out to be the most useless book you will ever buy. Because nothing in this book is something you don't know of.

This book is not going to be a revelation. It is meant to be a reminder. A reminder of how life happens to all of us, in a similar yet unequal fashion.

This book is not going to say something new. It is meant to put words to your thoughts. Thoughts that we all feel, repeatedly, but rarely stop to make sense of.

This book is not going to change your life. It is meant to make you more aware. So that you make choices in life from a state of awareness and not ignorance.

This book is a compilation of my thoughts that I have shared on social media over the past twelve months.

Most of which come from my own reflections, my own observations, my own experiences.

Back in school we used to play this game called book-cricket. Where we would open up a book to a random page, and the page number would determine how much we scored on that 'ball'. I imagine this book to be one such book-cricket, except we don't score runs. Instead, here we are reminded, we put words to our thoughts and we become more aware.

If I could make a suggestion, play book-cricket with this book.

Every day, open a random page. Read one, maybe three pages. Reflect upon them. Maybe make some notes. Or just smile at how it made you feel.

And then come back to it the next day.

If on any day you find yourself saying 'I needed to hear this today', consider me the bestselling author of the century!

stay awesome
stay focused
do epic shit!

PART 1

SUCCESS
(AND FAILURE)

My relationship with success has been driven largely by my relationship with multiple failures.

The mistakes that I have committed 'relentlessly' over the years.

The failures that I sat down with and reflected upon, that made me inch towards success at the most unexpected times.

This part of success isn't necessarily about prescriptions on how to get **successful**. It is rather about defining what success really means to you, staying true to that, and then using failures as reflections to create your own success!

Nothing beats the feeling of having done more in twenty-four hours than what the day expected you to!

You planned to do five tasks this morning.
Ended up doing seven.
With more productivity.
And far greater energy.

That joy, that emotion, when you've exceeded your own self, is true achievement.

Breaking your limits without even expecting to is the powerful way to see how much more you are capable of.

Others' success will
generate massive
self-doubt every
morning when you
get up.
Get up anyway.

. . .

A year from now, you will wish you had started today.

Start today.

Time goes away and leaves us with only one of these two things: regret or results.

A year from now you will wish you had unfollowed emotionally draining people.
A year from now you will wish you had said 'no' more often.
A year from now you will wish you had said 'yes' to yourself more often.

A year from now, you will never be sure of the results.
But you can certainly be sure of regret, if you don't start today.

What is the single biggest thing you can do to help you towards professional success?

People do not have to follow up, when you commit to doing something.

That's it.

. . .

How we think of our problems is how the world will think of our problems.

If we exaggerate our problems, so will the world.
If we are happy despite our problems, the world will help us get happier.

While we (almost always) don't choose our problems, we can always choose how to respond.

When we rule ourselves, we can never be ruled by our problems.

The biggest
misconception people
have is that they
are the odd one out
and everyone else is
sorted!

You are what you do.
Not what you say you'll do.

We know ourselves through our thoughts.
But we know others through their actions.

That is true for others as well.
They can't read our thoughts. All they see is
what we do.

It does not matter what we say.
What matters is what they see us doing.

Commitments are nothing if not backed up
with actions.

Luck happens to those that make things happen.

If you start creating content, you have greater chances of it being shared by your dream celebrity.

If you say hello to every stranger, you have greater chances of finding your dream partner. If you send cold emails every day, you have greater chances of getting your dream job!

Your actions decide your luck. So does your lack of actions.
Luck isn't really good fortune.
Luck is what eventually happens when your hard work yields results.

Persistence isn't a one-day miracle.

It is a conscious choice translated into habit.

The first few episodes of the Netflix series maybe boring. However, you still keep watching the series. It turns out, a friend told you to stay at it because it gets interesting eventually.

What if we treat our goals and our journey in the same way?

Keep at them, even when they are boring early on, because they will get interesting eventually?

The result of no efforts is nothing.
The result of persistent efforts is a habit where you cannot not do the right thing.

We have just one life.

Why live it with just one identity?

Why can't you be an entrepreneur who also creates content?
Why can't you have a day job and also sell your paintings on Instagram?
Why can't you be a professional sports person along with applying for B-schools?

We crave novelty, yet settle for a one-career life.
We crave novelty, yet choose to define ourselves by just one role, one title, one function, one designation.

We have one life.
But we don't need to be one person.

Consistency + Authenticity is the magic formula to crack the content game.

The content game magically helps you when:
- You are creating content at regular times (daily/thrice a week/weekly)
- You are You. You do not have to be someone else

This makes you enjoy the process. You find the hard work easy, and it becomes effortless for you, while everyone wonders how hard it must be!

If you are not authentic, you will struggle to be consistent.

No one can put up a façade for long!

True, not just for content.

True, for life!

The world will constantly be defining success and failure for you. Realizing this is what is called self-awareness.

Got a job. Success.
Got a job with CTC less than the neighbour's. Failure.

Got married by 25. Success.
Got divorced by 30. Failure.

The truth is, your current rules of success and failure have been written by the world.
Go ahead and rewrite them.
For yourselves.

If you stay true to them, it doesn't matter whether you are a failure according to the world.

If you don't stay true to them, it doesn't matter if you are a success according to the world.

Success is a relationship you have with your own self.

If you are unhappy with where you are in life right now, do not wait to find out what you should be doing.

Move out of where you are in life!

Set out on that exploration.
Don't wait to identify a destination.

Moving out doesn't mean quitting what you have. It means giving yourself the space to explore other things.

If you are in a job that you hate, but it pays you well, stay in the job but move out mentally and emotionally. Make it your job to find new opportunities.

The pro is the amateur who simply showed up every day.

No one is born a pro.
The pro is the amateur who put in their reps.
The pro is the amateur who fell in love with the process.
The pro is the amateur who chose practice and sleep over binge-watching.
The pro is the amateur who worked hard even when they had zero audience.
The pro is the amateur who persisted even when nothing seemed like it was working.

The pro is the amateur who refused to be called an amateur. And chose to let their hard work do the talking.

The pro is the one who chose discipline.

Over excuses.

Even when you know things may never be the same again, apologize.

Because you should.

You know you are not going to be forgiven.
Still, you should.
Because that is the right thing to do.

That is what the other person seeks.
That is what our role is, for the other person in the relationship.

You may not be wrong according to you. Yet, if apology is what makes others have their redemption, it is the right thing to do.

Doing what is right never comes with reasons. Because the right thing is the ultimate reason.

Don't measure how valuable you are by the way you are treated.

The world is going to treat you how it wishes to treat you.
You don't control that.
You only get to choose who you listen to.

If you measure your worth by those who don't treat you well, you are choosing to do so.
There is someone out there who values you.
Starting with your own self.

**Whatever you are feeling today will
fade away.**

That thing you imagine is the worst
thing ever?

When it happens, it will feel like that.

You will get up every day and it will be the
first thing you will think of.

Until one day, when it won't be!

No matter how happy you are, how sad you
are, you are not going to remember how
happy or sad you were, tomorrow.

Our emotions and feelings are temporary.
We think of them as permanent.

What you think is the worst thing in your life
isn't the worst thing.

Most sports are not played on the field.

They are played in the mind!

The best sportspeople have coaches who work on their mind training.
Playing amidst the pressure of millions of eyeballs.
Performing despite the media frenzy.
Doing their best even when they're going through a heartbreak.

Sports aren't only physical. Because anyone can get physically tough.

Sports mostly involve mental game. No one sees it. Only you.

It's the victory, the control of the mind, the joy of deciding what to focus on that leads to victory on the sports field.

The inner world drives the external one. Always.

The biggest roadblock to learning is ego!

Your ego keeps you from asking questions to those younger than you.

I must know everything!
How could I be so naïve?
It's impossible that I can't do it without asking them!

Ego is a bubble. Instead of bursting it and seeing what all lies outside, we invest most of our energy protecting it.

To know what you don't know is power.

To ask and learn what you don't know is a superpower.

When you say you have five years of experience, is it five years of experience or one year of experience done five times over?

Doing the same thing over and over years does not make you gain experience in those years. Doing different things, things out of your comfort zone, to stay curious, to never rest on your laurels, to expand what you know – these truly sum up experience.

Living as a template because it's comfortable isn't experience. It is choosing to not have experience.

The only template you need to follow is learning how to bulge out of your comfort zone. That's it! Every other template is a prison cell designed to make your life harder in the name of comfort.

Don't get comfortable.

Finding a mentor is a journey everyone should embark upon.

Don't place the burden on one person to be your mentor.

Have multiple mentors for different aspects of your life.

Don't think of mentors as only those who are much older and experienced.

The ones who have recently gone through, or are going through what you are going through, might have a lot more to offer in terms of perspective.

When you pick mentors who are way beyond your level of expertise, you might miss out on a lot. The things that you seek are so obvious to them they won't even realize you need an explanation!

When you pick mentors who are the same age and experience band as yours, they understand your problems. They highlight your issues. And offer suggestions based on what they wish they had. Not what they will become ten years hence.

Different life aspects. Different mentors. At the same time. Mostly, who have *recently* gone through what you are going through.

Most people treat picking mentors as picking sandwiches at your nearby Michelin Star-rated restaurant. Picking them because they have been in place for the last ten years.

Picking mentors truly is like picking your Subway sandwich. You get to decide everything.

'It is not my job'

= death for a startup

= survival for a large company

In a startup, you may don multiple hats because it's a small company.

The mindset of 'It's not my job' restricts you. Because now you are living in boundaries that don't even exist.

In a large company, everyone is specialized in their roles.

The mindset of 'It's not my job' mostly helps you because it would enable the one doing their job to do it well.

You don't find your passion.

You grow your passion!

Passion is not something that makes you M.F. Hussain or A.R. Rahman or Sachin Tendulkar on Day 1.

Passion is that tiny inner nudge to paint, compose music or play cricket – the nudge that refuses to leave you, till the time you nurture it daily.

Passion is persistence, because that is the reason you are still in it despite all the reasons to quit.

Passion is showing up to do the work, no matter how good you're at it already.

Passion is signing up for hard work, because not choosing it would be harder!

It is crazy how many people take decisions relying on their heart, when it should be an Excel sheet they should be relying on!

It is crazy how many people take decisions relying on an Excel sheet, when it should be their heart they should be relying on!

The decisions about money are best made through an Excel sheet.

The decisions about people are best made with your heart.

We were ALL born with the innate ability to ask questions. Endlessly.

And then school and parents kill it!

There was nothing wrong with us as kids.

Except our environment that told us that asking questions is a wrong thing.

Don't ask silly questions.
Shut your mouth.
That's dumb!!

FALSE!

It's okay to ask questions.
It's okay to be genuinely curious to know more.
It's more than okay to ask even if others would think it is 'dumb'.

You may have numbed yourself because it was not cool to be curious, it helps to know that nurturing your curiosity cat is the coolest thing in a world where people are scared of being called dumb.

Once you succeed, people see only success.
If you fail, they see only failure.

They don't see the journey. Only you do. It is on this journey that your life was lived!

No one sees the multiple failures before that one 'huge success'.

No one sees how you overcame your habits and systems despite having 'failed', because they focus on the end result, that you failed.

What you become during the process of success and failure is what's most important.

No one else would see it.
Only you would.

So be it, because that is your true life. Success or failure happened as a result. What you did and who you became was your life in true essence.

'Success and failure' were merely outputs. What you carry in your heart to reach that destination is conclusive.

If you often worry about what people will think of you, you will often end up doing what people want you to do.

If you worry that people won't like your decisions, you will make decisions that would please them.

If you do not care about people's opinions, you would finally do what you want to.

Thinking about what people think of you is living in a prison cell with bars only in front of you. There is open space for you to run on the sides, yet what you choose is staying behind those bars.

The simple formula to get out of those bars? Ask yourself: 'What do *I want*?'

3 relationships
that define almost
everything that
happens to us in
our lives.

- The relationship we
  have with money.

- The relationship we
  have with time.

- The relationship we
  have with ourselves.

No one expects a CA to make a visually colourful résumé.
No one expects a musician to send an Excel sheet proposal.
No one expects an engineer to send a video résumé.

Which is why they should consider doing it!

Fighting the stereotype is a great way to get attention!

If you send a résumé that is not 'how your résumé must be' but rather 'how you are', most companies would react in two ways:

- They'd either hate it
- Or they'd remember you

Both are good signs, as now the companies select going by who is worthy of you and which ones are those you shouldn't be working with.

'What if I get rejected?' But what if you get rejected from the place where you are supposed to be an original and you tried to fit in by sending a standard résumé?

Being yourself is the coolest way to get attention. Which is scary for most people. Which is the reason most people don't.

There is temporary discomfort in doing the unconventional.

There is permanent discomfort in living life as a template.

It is going to be scary and uncomfortable walking your own path.

Guess what's even more scary? To walk by the path that everyone walks on, only to realize you never wanted to walk on that path.

It is indeed a lot of resistance to break the chains of convention and do your own thing. However, it saves you from a ton of inner resistance for the rest of your life – allowing for the path you could take, the regrets you could avoid, and the joy you could accomplish. Just by doing the unconventional and resisting the obvious.

You can be yourself and be rebuked for a year.

Or you can be someone else and never face yourself in the mirror.

Why choose the latter when the former is the easy springboard to jump away from the herd?

While you are
building your skills,
the most important
thing to build is your
reputation.

Your goal is to make
people say: 'I am not
sure if she knows
how to do it. But I am
certain if told to do
it, she will definitely
figure it out. I trust
her.'

Mistakes I made in my 20s

Mistake 1

I continued to pursue my education because I was good at it, without ever asking myself if it made me happy.

Just because you are good at something doesn't automatically ensure you are happy doing it.

Mistake 2

I looked down upon people who used to smoke or drink or party every weekend.

I felt they were losers and the reason to bring the world down.

It is not what you do but who you are underneath that defines you.

Mistake 3

I read books that made me look cool. Without truly understanding what I could learn from those books, until much later in life.

People do not remember you for the company you keep.

They remember you for who you become because of that company.

Mistake 4

I felt morally obligated to help everyone in distress.

And if they continued to remain unhappy, I blamed myself.

The best gift you can give yourself and to others is to take care of your own happiness.

Mistake 5

I felt the lack of money was the root cause of all our family problems.

And once we have money, we would no longer have any problems.

Our problems are the stories we tell ourselves of how everything will be fine once we get what we want.

Mistake 6

I felt that rich kids would never make it in life because they got everything on a platter and did not know how to struggle.
Their privilege would always harm them.

It is not the privilege that harms us.
It is our lack of awareness of our own privilege that harms us.

Mistake 7

I ate shit, slept odd hours, maintained bad posture while constantly telling myself that I have tomorrow to fix all of this.

An excuse is the distance between who you are and who you wish to be.

Mistake 8

I really tried hard to please people. I wanted them to like me, to think highly of me, to speak highly of me.

If your happiness depends on external validation, then your happiness depends on something you do not control.

Mistake 9
I took loans.
Because I didn't have money yet.

And I kept telling myself, 'But I will have money in the future. And that's why it is okay.'

If you do not have the money to pay for something right now, you DO NOT have the money.

Mistake 10
I didn't think subjective topics such as psychology, business ethics or human resources were needed or even important.

Business is all about finance and marketing.
Business is all about people.
How well you know them.
And how you treat them.

Mistake 11

I assumed if I speak well and speak confidently, it would cover up for the lack of content I have.

You cannot lie on stage.
The audience will always know what is within your heart.

Mistake 12

If people approached me with their problems, my job was to determine whether the problem was worth my time or not.

And if it was, then my job was to fix it.

Listening to someone without judgement or prescription is the most precious gift you can give someone.

Mistake 13

I need to have a plan.
A plan is the only way to get to any point in life.

If you do not have a plan, you do not have any chance of getting anywhere.

To not have a plan and be okay with it is the best plan.

Mistake 14
I looked around and saw that everything was designed to make our lives comfortable.
And so I assumed the purpose of life was to make life comfortable.

Avoiding the comfort trap is the difference between who you are and who you could have been.

Mistake 15
If I said something, wrote something, shared something, I felt dejected when no one cared, when no one responded, when no one commented.

No one owes you their time and money. You earn it, every day, by the work you do.

Mistake 16

I had to make money fast, buy my parents that house, buy that fancy car, that vacation. I had to make money fast, to buy stuff.

Money can buy you stuff. But the biggest thing it buys is freedom.
Including freedom from stuff.

Mistake 17

I assumed if you work hard, really hard, you would eventually win.
Working hard is the only thing that matters.

What you work on is just as important as how much you work on it.
Even donkeys work hard.
Working smart is the difference between a donkey and a human.

Mistake 18

I blamed myself for being late in the game.
At 29 I was jobless with no money, no plan and no clue.

I remember looking at Mark Zuckerberg and feeling shitty! :)

Everyone is running a different race.
In fact, we're not even in a race.
We're on our own paths.
Some walk. Some run.

Mistake 19
I assumed my work would speak for me.
If I did well, people would give me what I deserved and what I wanted.
I never asked for what I wanted!

If you don't ask, the answer is always no.

Ninety per cent of what happened to me in my 20s was because of luck.

I am that guy who was at the right place at the right time and lucked out. And as much as I am grateful for that, I wish I had known better.

Today I know, the 20s should be used to discover yourself, as against stabilizing yourself.

Meet as many people as you can, do as many jobs as you can, explore as many streams as you can.
Find out what you are good at and what makes you happy.

And then spend your 30s doing that.
I am embarrassed at who I was in my 20s.

The underconfident, people-pleasing, overweight, stuck on one path, bad with money, judgmental kid.

But I am glad I was all of that.
Because now I know who I do not want to be.

'I wish everyone could get rich and famous and everything they ever dreamed of so they can see that's not the answer.'

– Jim Carrey

Mistakes I made in my 30s

Mistake 1
I hired people with strong pedigree and great brands on their résumé, ignoring how they operated as people.
I assumed their degrees would drive their success.

As you grow professionally, it is not what you know but how you deal with people that determines your success.

Mistake 2
I told myself that relationships can wait.

That call to my parents can wait.
Saying 'I love you' to my wife and kids can wait.
Spending time with them without my phone can wait.

I told myself, 'I don't have the time.'

Time is the only thing that matters.
Everything else can wait.

Mistake 3
I managed everyone the same way.
My way.

The way that was easy for me, scalable for me, convenient for me.
If there is anything that should not scale with size, it is leadership.
It should get harder for you to lead, as you grow.

Because people are different.
They are not you!

Mistake 4
I felt having a second child would be a disaster.
It would make me feel even more guilty for not being present as a father to our son.

When you don't have anyone, you have your siblings.

And that's something you don't ask for.
Your parents give you that gift.

Mistake 5
I put all my savings into illiquid assets – real estate, startups.
And when we went through financial turmoil, we lived like urban poor.
Selling jewellery to make ends meet.

It is easy to cut a cheque.
Only when you see money come of it, do you call it an investment!

Mistake 6
I assumed everyone's definition of and motivation for success is the same.
That of glory. That of respect. That of inspiring others.

Everyone has a different definition of success.
And only if your work sets other people up for their success will you be successful yourself.

Mistake 7

After the birth of our first child, I felt I lost my partner to my son's mother.
I missed my friend, my confidante.
Because she was always busy rearing our child.

It is only when both parents contribute in raising their child that they keep their partnership alive.

Mistake 8

I felt bad once all the awards stopped coming my way, after I started nearbuy.
When I had an easy job at Groupon, I was spoken of.
When I worked the hardest ever, no one noticed.

The awards are never for us.
They are for the positions we hold.

Mistake 9

I felt venture capitalists were in the business of building businesses together with the founders.

And our interests were thus aligned.

Venture capitalists are in the business of entering and exiting businesses.

And that often means the interests will eventually clash.

Mistake 10

I was convinced I would do well financially, if I became an entrepreneur.

I would raise tons of money and be worth millions.

Never start up because you want to make money from it.

The odds of making the same money through a 'boring' professional career is much higher.

Mistake 11
I assumed people would be okay if we laid them off and found them another job.
No!

Laying people off is rarely about the job. It is about their self-respect.

Mistake 12
I maxed my credit cards, borrowed money from friends, delayed my payments, just so I could continue to maintain the lifestyle that I had.
I felt going down on that was a sign of failure.

Treating our lifestyle standards as a measure of our success is a sign of failure.

Mistake 13:
I thought that no one wants to be led. Everyone wants to do their own thing, so let them.
Not true.

Ninety-nine per cent of people want to be led. They want to be told what to do, and then they will go on to do their best.

They want to be led. Not managed.

Mistake 14
I allowed my irrational optimism about the future take over the need to be deliberate and thoughtful before making decisions.
I assumed an 'everything will be ok' approach towards everything.

Hope is not a strategy.

In my 20s, I dropped out of my PhD, finished an MBA, worked in consulting earning a lot, started up with some success, had founder conflicts that led me to leave.

At 29, I was jobless, with no money, no plans and no visibility.

But I learnt a lot.

In my 30s, I started 2 businesses, raised money, laid off people, made absolutely no money for myself and my investors, made poor people decisions, and wasn't a good father.

At 39, I was again jobless, with no money, no plans and no visibility.

But I wouldn't have it any other way.
I am fortunate that my 30s were much better than my 20s, when it comes to the mistakes that I made and the impact they had on me.

As the decade passed, I realized what is truly important in life.

It wasn't money for me, or fame or recognition. It was the ability to do what I wanted to, without caring about what the world thinks of me.

I made a lot of mistakes on my way to arrive at this definition of success.

And I consider myself fortunate.
If it weren't for these mistakes, I would still be an ill-aware 41-year-old adult, who knows nothing better than a 5-year-old does!

Reflecting upon my mistakes has taught me the most about myself.

I hope it does the same magic for you too:)

My failure résumé

I turned 41 in 2021.
Here is a list of things I have failed at.

My failure résumé

Getting into the IITs was a dream.
I tried it during my 12th.
Didn't make it.
Not even close.

It was the first time I saw my father cry.
I am guessing he felt this would be the one
that will get us out of our financial miseries.

I don't know.
I never asked him why he cried that day.

I didn't make it to any engineering college.
None that mattered, that I wanted to get into.

So, I decided to go for a three-year BSc
degree.

From St Stephens.
I was rejected at the interview stage.

Dr Wilson said, 'I don't think you will be good in Physics.'

Tried again for the IITs while in first year of college.
Didn't make it.
Not even close.
This time no one cried.
Not even me.
Maybe I knew it all along.

Once college was over, I decided to go to the IITs for my master's in Physics.
Sat for the exams.
Didn't make it to any, except IIT Kanpur, which called me for an interview.

Dr H.C. Verma asked me a question.
I didn't even know how to begin to answer.

I apologized and left the room.
Began applying to the US Universities for my PhD in Physics.
Princeton was the top university that I wanted to get into.
Applied to seven universities in all.

Within a month, six of them had rejected me.
Joined the only university that accepted me.

One particular course's final exam.
The professor asked the rationale behind a theorem.
I vomited the entire proof.
No errors.

Heard back.
'Haven't seen anyone remember this so well. I wonder how much of it you truly understand?'

Dropped out of my PhD.
Came back to India.
Everyone was devastated.

I was 24.
No money.
No plan.
No direction.
No career.
No education.

Decided to do an MBA, to change directions.
Sat for CAT, to get into the IIMs.
Didn't make it to the interview shortlist of any
of them.
None!

Got into Indian School of Business (ISB) (till
date do not know how or why).

Figured consulting is what will give me the
most exposure, considering I didn't have any
experience to be proud of.

Applied to all consulting firms.
Everyone rejected, except Boston Consulting
Group (BCG) and A.T. Kearney.

Sat for the BCG interview.

The interviewer at the end of the conversation asked, 'How much would you rate your performance today on a scale of 5?'

'2/5, I guess.'

'I'd agree,' he replied.

For my first project in consulting, I was to build a detailed business plan for a real estate client.

I hated accounting.

And did a sloppy job of it.

Every draft was laden with mistakes.

'If I can't trust you with your work, it doesn't matter how smart you are,' my manager remarked.

Joined my MBA batch mate in his startup, as a co-founder.

I didn't use technology to scale, kept fighting problems with my time, didn't admit my

mistakes, didn't seek feedback, didn't think I
was doing anything wrong.
After a year he fired me.
He did the right thing.

I was 29.
No money.
No plan.
No direction.

Decided to take up a job and thought product
management was the right role for me.
Applied to Google and Facebook.
Never heard back from either.

Decided to start up instead.
A food company.
Pitched to Indian Angel Network, Mumbai
Angels. And 11 High Net-Worth Individuals.
Everyone rejected the idea.
At that time, I thought everyone rejected me.

Got the opportunity to run some of Groupon's APAC markets.
Didn't know how to delegate.
Didn't know how to lead from a distance.
Didn't know how to get results through others.

Failed miserably as a leader and manager.

Got the opportunity to buy Groupon's India business by raising external capital.
Pitched to 23 venture capitalists across the world.
Twenty-two said no.

Launched a referral programme on nearbuy, without the checks and balances.
Lost Rs 11 crore in a month!
Thought the growth, even if unprofitable, would excite investors.
So money would eventually come.

Running fast out of money, we had to reduce our burn.

Laid off 80 people out of 300.
Stood in front of the company apologizing and crying.
I had failed everyone.
And myself.

In my irrational optimism we had signed up for a much larger office than required, after the buyout.
With no money, we began sub-leasing the office.
Once the lease expired, we had to vacate.
Leaving our tenants high and dry.
They thought we would never leave.
I did too.

Began the process of fund-raising again.
Pitched to 68 investors across the world.
Sixty-seven refused.
One gave us a term sheet.
And withdrew before we signed.

All this while, we took salary cuts to reduce our losses.
And my personal expenses were greater than the income.
I had no savings.
All my savings had been invested in nearbuy.

I had to borrow from friends.
Both my credit cards maxed out.

I had to keep my parent's house as collateral to raise money for my sister's wedding.
To gift Vidur a bicycle on his birthday, something he had been asking for a year, we had to sell Ruchi's gold bangles.

We surprised him when he came from school.
He broke down.
So did we.

Despite my best intentions, nearbuy could not become what I had imagined it to be.

Investors lost their money.
People lost their jobs.
So many lost their confidence and trust.
I failed to make it work.
And realized I should not attempt to, any more.

I was 39.
No money.
No plan.
No direction.

A résumé is such an interesting document.
It is a showcase of all the great things you have done, accomplished and are proud of.
But it never talks about how you reached there.

The failures that got you there.
My life is so much more about my failures than any of the little things I have managed to accomplish.

For the first six years of his life, Vidur used to draw the family with me holding a phone in my hand.

That is how he remembered his father.

My parents didn't hear from me for days, because I was busy. Trying to make amends around my other failures in life, not realizing that through this I was carving out yet another failure.

My investors and colleagues trusted me, with their money, their careers, their time.
And I failed to keep their trust intact.
I played with their money, their careers, their trust.
Always hoping that I could do something to redeem myself and get it all back.
But it didn't happen.

And that is my failure.
And that is my story.

I am so so blessed to have lived my life.

Would I go back and change anything?
Most likely not.

I wish I had acted better, been better, done
better in the past, but I wouldn't have it any
other way.
I am who I am because of these failures.

The scars that you wear on your body.
Don't regret them.
Don't hate them.
Don't reject them.

They are signs of a battle you fought.
And even if you lost, the scars were left behind
as a reminder of who you were and who you
can be.

At the end of the day, when you undress
yourself, the scars tell a story that only you
know.

Don't wish for more scars.
But surely be aware of the ones you have.

Perhaps one day you will be proud of them as well.

PS1:
It is easy for someone to assume that where I ended up in life (colleges, companies, investors, etc.) were not my first choices and hence were not the right choices.

That is not true.

I was rejected by everyone. But those colleges, companies and investors accepted me. They are no less in my eyes. Never!

PS2:
I am insanely lucky. So lucky that it shocks me at times.
So, it might be easy to conclude that all of this

is humblebrag and I have actually enjoyed a lot of success.

My success remains unexplained. I cannot justify it nor can I claim it.

PART 2
HABITS

For the longest time, I have been a student of habits.

I don't set goals, for two reasons:
- You do it for a destination, instead of becoming someone in the process
- You invariably start chasing another destination, upon reaching one.

Instead, habits have come to help me in the smallest to biggest things in life.

Be it a habit of sleeping on time.

Or recording videos religiously for four-plus years, when no one was watching me.

Or writing my blog since 2005, which has somehow eventually led to this book.

I love habits, because the kind of person I become pursuing them opens up multiple doors, instead of chasing goals that may (perhaps) lead to just one door if one gets lucky.

Habits build us, goals lay us barren.

The trick to waking up early is not waking up early.
It is sleeping on time!

The secret is not merely waking up early. Any alarm clock could do that for you.
The secret is to be energized, happy and productive in the morning.

Nothing could ensure this other than sleeping on time.
Otherwise, what's the use of waking up early and feeling groggy and eventually hating yourself?

Waking up early fizzles out, sleeping on time is what flourishes.

Share your journey.
Document your journey.
Narrate your journey.

Your story is valuable.
Maybe you don't see it.

Think of it as a guide for someone who hasn't
yet gone through what you have.
If only you looked at yourself through the eyes
of the ones you inspired.

Every time you stop from sharing what you
know because 'who will listen to me; I am
nobody', some nobody is sharing what they
know and that becomes the 'gold standard'.

You have a moral responsibility to share.

Curiosity has created more opportunities than hard work ever will.

Why isn't my favourite startup founder creating content?
How could I add value to the person I'm writing a cold email to before asking them something in return?
Why not?

The key to having more opportunities in life is to give yourself enough opportunities to get curious.

You have no idea how the dumb questions that you avoid asking could solve someone's dilemma that they can't avoid!

Targets are the enemy of habits.

Don't set targets.
Set habits!

Setting targets instead of habits makes us forget the kind of person we want to become.

We not only want to run a marathon. We also want to get fit.
We not only want to look sculpted. We want to see how disciplined we are.
We do not want to crack just the sales numbers.
We want to solve more customer problems.

The more we get the process right, the closer we get to the targets.
The more we run after targets, the more we sign up for feeling hollow once we achieve them.

Habits hire us forever and take us higher, whereas targets tame us and leave us clueless after we achieve them.

Don't try to minimize your struggle.
Try to make it more meaningful.

You can never minimize your struggle. It will only suppress your emotions.
However, you can always figure out what it means.

Feeling intimidated by a colleague daily? Does it mean you aren't 'cool enough' or does it simply mean they do not make you feel involved?

Trying too hard to find work you love? Does this mean you aren't worth it or does it mean your efforts are compounding to give you 10X return?

Parents asking you for small things? Does this mean they are poking their nose or does this mean they simply want to lower their anxiety by making sure you're safe?

When we suppress struggle, it doesn't go away. It just bottles up making us question ourselves daily.

When we *choose* the meaning of our struggle, we use it instead of it using us.

Before you assume, try this crazy thing.

ASK!

Someone is ignoring you? Perhaps they are going through a tough time, and don't even know they are ignoring you. Why not ask?

People aren't good to you? Maybe they are trying to be good to themselves as well. Why not ask?

Want to talk to your parents? Maybe they want to, as well. Why not ask?

Asking is the best thing to do, before making assumptions.

It either validates your assumption or you get to understand people better. Either way, you get to be a better communicator.

Win-win :)

Most important skills today that are hardly taught:

Humour

Storytelling

Managing money

Human psychology

Cold emailing

You won't get out of laziness for something you don't want to do.

I wake up at 4:30 a.m. every morning. After meditating, singing practice and reading, I head to play tennis.

Daily.

Whether it is 36 degrees in June or 6 degrees in December. Just because I love it!

However, I might not do that to watch cricket on TV. Or I might not want to watch a trending series. I might certainly never make any effort to create a fixed deposit.

Only because I don't want to!

We don't need more productivity hacks. We need to spend more time with ourselves doing what we want to do.

The best form of writing is the one that is written neither out of fear nor with the willingness to share.

Write not because you want to be liked.
Write not because you want more likes.
Write not because someone else will be impressed by you.

Write, because you want to express yourself.
Write, because you will read it.
Write, because if you won't, your bottled-up emotions will harm you alone.
Write, because if you won't write it, how will you ever read what you need?
Write, because no one could ever be You 2.0.

To start the habit of reading books, read books that you will enjoy.

Not books that the world thinks you should be reading!

Three things that will tell you who/what you consider as important in your life.

1. Your first hour after you wake up

2. Your last hour before you sleep

3. Your calendar

The first 60 minutes of my day are me-time. I sip water like wine. Just smile at the blessings I have. Meditate.

The last 60 minutes of my day are family time. Either I read with Vidur, or I help Ruchi put Uzma to bed, before we catch up on our day. Lovely time!

Some of the things my calendar has that are super-important to me: Afternoon nap, 1:1 catch-ups with my team, reading time, music lessons, getting my daughter ready for the morning.

The things that are easy to do are also the things that are easy to ignore.
If you choose to do them with consistency instead of ignorance, they can change your life *completely*.

Daily progress isn't about becoming an expert in your field.

It is developing the mindset that progress is a way of life.

It is like breathing.

We rarely stop to acknowledge it.

But we breathe every second.

We would die without it.

Reading books will not make you smart.
Watching motivational videos will not make you driven.
Writing will not make your thoughts clearer.

We are not shaped by these things.
We are shaped by the stories we tell ourselves.

Reading books isn't the answer. The answer is what we take away from them.

Writing isn't the answer to clarity. The answer lies in whether we write to get more at peace or whether we write to seek validation.

Motivational videos certainly aren't the answer (even though I make a bunch every week). The video we turn our life into after watching those videos is the answer.

Nothing changes until we change what lives between our two ears.

**We know others through their actions.
We know ourselves through our thoughts.**

What others are thinking, we don't know. We only know what they are doing.
That is exactly what they see when they look at us – what we do, instead of what we think.

We may have a hundred plans, but, what others see is the one we are executing.
Plans don't work without performance.

Thoughts are powerful, when they are converted into actions.
Without action, they are simply broken promises.

We nod to show that we are listening.
But we are not listening to the opposite
person.
Instead, we are listening to our mind
telling us what to say.

When we listen, do we truly listen or are we
preparing a response in our heads?
When we listen, are we coming with an open
mind, or just a closed book that knows all the
answers?
When we listen, do we intend to help or do we
just want to impose our point of view?

We nod to show we are listening to respond.
However, what if we nodded to purely listen
to what others have to truly convey?
What if we nodded to understand what's
coming in, instead of structuring what we had
already planned?

Your attendance doesn't define your discipline.

Your attention does.

College requires you to have certain attendance.
Some companies want you to be in the office for attendance.
Worse, even relatives want you to be present at parties you hate!

What if you are present, but not happily present?
You'll be lost, hating everyone, and hating your life.

Your discipline is defined when you are fully present, for all the times you are present.
That shows you are interested, enjoying the process, and in the flow!

The quality of your presence is way more important than the forced quantity of your attendance when you're not present.

Who you spend time with will define the stories you hear.

The stories you hear will define the stories in your head.

The stories in your head will define you.

Choose who you spend time with, wisely!

Optimize for learning, not salary.
Optimize for progress, not stability.
Optimize for facing fears, not for comfort.

If you have two job offers with a similar salary, the one with growth is the one you want to pick up.

If you really want stability in terms of money and career, no one gets it unless they embrace progress as their way of life.

Comfort stems from facing what you fear. Staying in the comfort zone is the most dangerous thing to do.

The things that are the easiest to do are the things that are the hardest to live with.
Yet they are the only things that make our life easier.

As a fresher, you do not have a hope in hell of getting noticed.

Just work, don't ask questions, don't challenge, say yes to your boss, don't try to be too friendly.

The key is to stick around.

And lie low.

Just one of the many lies told to us.

Some of the smartest people in the world are competing for your sleep time.

You know what that means?

Your sleep is VERY IMPORTANT!

to you AND to them.

Don't let them win!

The social media and streaming platforms are designed in a manner that hooks your attention.

More you like the content
More they will recommend it.
More watch time. Less sleep time.

Disconnection helps, because motivation can't, especially if all the smartest minds of the world are 24x7 thinking on how to keep you glued.

Saying no to everything else and sleeping on time – is the greatest secret sauce of self-love.

Do not allow comfort to make you believe that you no longer need to try!

You've got a good job through hard work.
Shouldn't try to get better any more.

Having beautiful relationships with people you care for.
Shouldn't try to care for them any more.

Got a sculpted body after relentless hard work.
Shouldn't try to maintain it any more.

Wrong.

Comfort is a destination.
Trying more is a path.
To get to the next level of destination of comfort.

If we stay stuck in just one destination (comfort), we forget our home (happiness).

Happiness certainly never comes through staying cool in what seems comfortable.

Happiness is simply a result of slaying your comfort, so you always stay comfortable staying out of your comfort zone.

No step is small, as long as it is headed in the direction of where we want to go.

In a society that is obsessed with hard work and career success, seeking boredom is an act of rebellion.

Seeking boredom through free time helps you feel comfortable in your skin.

Seeking boredom in your own company makes you not crave for anyone else's company.

Seeking boredom in the relentless daily habits makes you create success automatically.

We want success and work hard to get there, hardly ever knowing that the hardest work is to seek ease in the mundane.

Find it hard to say no
to people, when you
know you should?

It's mostly because
you worry about what
they will think of you.

If you follow the right set of people on social media, opportunities will come by design.

Not by luck!

You become like the people you spend your time with – online and offline.
Approaching life questions.
Complaining or figuring out solutions.
Saying no to new things or asking 'what if' and 'why not'.

They are a result of the choices we've made to follow people online.

And it's almost impossible to not have great opportunities because following the right people teaches you how to create your life around having new opportunities.

A sneak peek into my habits

While you now know what I think about habits,
here is how habits think through me.
A sneak peek, into my habits.

Habit 1

I always carry a notebook with me.

I take notes like a school student.
I put tasks in a calendar.
I send myself emails in the future.

My mind's energy should be spent in thinking.
Not remembering!

Habit 2

Document EVERYTHING!

At any point I have three notebooks
1. Ideas.
2. To-do lists for the day.
3. Meeting notes.

And I write things down.

Writing helps tell the brain that this is important.
And it helps me not to 'try and remember' anything.

Habit 3
I put everything on a calendar.

My calendar is my lifeline.
Everything is on my calendar.
Bills to pay, birthdays to remember, threads to write, weekly routines.

Over fifty per cent of my waking time goes towards things that are important, but not urgent! :)

Habit 4
I schedule emails to myself, for the future.

There are so many things that interest me, that it becomes important to prioritize.

And for me prioritization is about scheduling.
Future emails serve that purpose.

Habit 5
Using technology for everything possible.

There are a lot of tasks that suck your time,
but do not make you move forward.
Consider using technology to solve them for
you.

Habit 6
Sharing my calendar with my wife.

I kid you not, this is a game changer.
She has hundred per cent access, so she can
add, edit and delete things from my calendar.
So I do not have to think about anything when
it comes to family events, birthdays, or even
things she wants me to do.

She simply adds it to my calendar.
Productivity MAX!

Habit 7

I have two WhatsApp self-groups.

Create a group on WhatsApp with someone.
Once done, delete that someone else.
Now it's just you in the group.
Pin that group to the top.
And use it for easy sharing and access.

1. Docs/Images
   Which is where I store my important images (PAN Card, License Copy, passport copy, etc.) and documents for easy access (tickets, etc.).

2. Thoughts
   Which I use to just type something on the run, or click something, or record/shoot something.

Habit 8
Afternoon nap is my daily ritual.

I grew up in a home where Ma insisted, we sleep for an hour after lunch.
I guess that's just stayed.

Then I remember going to China and Korea and saw that in offices, too, there was a culture of an afternoon nap (heads down on the table)
Never implemented it in nearbuy, but did implement it personally.
I used to grab 15 minutes of a power nap while in the office. And since I stepped down from nearbuy, I have tried to nap for an hour.

My daughter and I sleep together. Nothing feels better :)

Habit 9
Setting the right environment is super-important.

I never work from my bed, always on a table.
I never read lying down, always on a chair.
I never eat while watching something.
I never work in a dark room. Always natural light.

Even when it is work from home, change into 'office attire' while working and not be in your PJs – subconsciously tricks your mind to get into the comfort zone!

Do not underestimate your surroundings while trying to create flow!

Habit 10
Create sensory hooks for what is important (not what is urgent).

As a species, our senses have evolved to work for us. What we see, smell, touch, hear and taste, drives almost all of our reactions.

I use my senses to drive action.

Keep your phone in another room while sleeping.

Place your dumb-bells right next to your bed.

Keep the book where you can see it easily.

Set your alarm to that song that lifts you up.

Apply your favourite deo/perfume when starting the day.

These things work!

As the world progresses, it is getting easier to slump into laziness and feel lethargic.
And it is getting equally easier to lift yourself out of slumber and get moving.

It is frankly a matter of intent.
Not capability any more.
Not even access.

The human mind is conditioned to feel happy and fulfilled while making progress.

Set your life in such a manner that you can measure this progress.

Even a tiny improvement in your productivity will yield results over time.

PART 3
AWARENESS

E ach time someone asks me what would my advice be, to my 20-year-old self, I have one answer:

'Make sure decisions in your life are made from a point of view of awareness and not ignorance.'

Everything I do online is to help people make better choices through making them more aware.

That's what I tell my team as well. We aren't creating content. We are creating awareness which helps people make better decisions.

Hope my takes on awareness in the succeeding pages will help you get there.

If everyone did it, it wouldn't need to be said.

Not everyone exercises. Thus, it needs to be said more often.
Not everyone spends time with their team. Thus, the best leaders say it more often.
Not everyone spends time journaling. Thus, the wisest minds help us to get into the habit.

Everyone watches TV, it needn't be said.
Everyone eats pizza, it needn't be said.
Everyone has a smartphone, it needn't be said, possess one.

The things that are the most important and the least practised, are the things that are said.
Doing the things that are the most important are the things that make you important.

Most of my decisions in life were not made because of my confidence in the decision.
They were made because of my awareness of the situation.

I wasn't sure if dropping out of my PhD was a good decision.
I wasn't sure if going to ISB was a good one either.
Nor was I sure if giving up a corporate job for a startup was right.

I wasn't sure if they were the right decisions.

However, what I knew for sure was that I was not ready to continue with things as they were.
I knew I had to make those decisions because I had explored all other options.
I knew I had to make those decisions because I would regret not making them later.

I didn't know whether those decisions were right or wrong.

However, not making those decisions despite being aware of all other options was certainly the wrong decision.

Decisions are not for decoding destinations. Decisions are for deciphering the path you want to demonstrate next.

Our actions are driven by our feeling of what people feel about us!
This begs the question, whose life are we living?

We take actions to oblige others, when we don't want to.
When we hate our day job and have set aside the weekend for a job we like, we instead go out with friends.
We go to parties when we are trying to set up a fixed bed-time.

We say yes more often just because we want people to feel good about us!

We thus end up feeling worse because of these tiny betrayals.

In a world filled with people living their lives for someone else, a truly well-lived life, is the one where we stay true to our own selves.

That's difficult. But not an inch more difficult than living someone else's life.

Emotional debt has killed more people than financial debt ever will.

The debt of never saying 'I love you' to your parents.
The debt of never apologizing to the friend who was always there for you.
The debt of never living for your happiness, because you were busy pleasing others.

Money goes and comes.
We might be in a position to pay those debts off one day.
However, the emotional debt that piles on, will continue to kill us within every single day we live!

If unsure between two choices, picking both is almost always the wrong response.

Do you want money or power?
Do you want an awesome college or an awesome course?
Should you go after the salary or after the brand?

You can say both.
And live a life of compromise or indecision.

Or you can choose the one which you want to do.
And succeed at it.
Or if you didn't succeed, learn from the courage you displayed.

Picking one, teaches.
Picking both, confuses.

Being calm is a skill.

Being calm when you are ridiculed.
Being calm when you are left alone.
Being calm when you are questioned.

Not because they were right. Perhaps they were. Perhaps they were not.
Because, if you lose your calm, you compound the unpleasant further instead of correcting it.

Anyone can be calm when things are calm.
Being calm despite the storm is a powerful skill.

Just because someone carries it well doesn't mean it isn't heavy.

Everyone carries a heavy load.

Be kind to others.

Fear has led to more procrastination than laziness ever will.

You don't procrastinate because you are lazy. You procrastinate because you are scared.

What if I fail?
What if I succeed?
What if my life is sorted after this?
What if I have to face rejection?

You aren't lazy. You simply aren't ready to meet yourself on the other side.
Because you won't have those reasons then, and living a fearless life isn't what you are used to.

Finding security in your own achievement is the biggest achievement.

Someone younger than you is always going to be making more money than you.
That's the truth.

However, no matter how much success you achieve, if you are still envious, are you truly successful?

The world despises satisfaction. I believe satisfaction is the most powerful skill to have.

Satisfaction in your journey.
Satisfaction in how far you've come.
Satisfaction in all the unwanted parts of you you've scooped out.
Satisfaction in your satisfaction!

Only when you are truly satisfied, will you enjoy your journey on the other mountains to climb. Otherwise, you'll always be looking on the sides and overlooking the majestic view your own journey has!

Do not confuse calmness with a lack of fire.

Calmness doesn't mean lack of drive.
It rather means having the power to turn that drive into actions.

Calm people have the most fire, because they use their courage to do bold things. Instead of using up that fire to speak.

The calm IS the fire.
Because that is the fire that brings ideas to execution.
Thoughts to action.
And tangents to tangibles.

Your self-talk determines your self-worth.

We are all the stories we tell ourselves.

I'm a loser! I can never wake up early! I can never get along with people!!

OR

If I take small steps, I can do it!
I am enough!
I have handled more difficult things in the past!

Every morning we wake up. To live a life that runs through our stories.
While looking at ourselves in the mirror.
We can change the story we tell ourselves.

Not making a decision because you are scared of making the wrong decision?

If you don't move, you would've already made the wrong decision.

When you make a decision, you will either succeed. Or you won't.
When you succeed, you will know how life works.
When you won't, you will learn a life-altering lesson.

Neither of this will happen if you stay where you are.

Movement brings momentum.
Stagnation amplifies sadness.

The best mental model for taking tough decisions in life?

1. Ask yourself, 'What's the worst thing that can happen?'
2. Close your eyes and vividly imagine it happening.
3. Then ask, 'Will I be okay – mentally, socially, financially, physically, emotionally?'

If yes, go for it.

Who is the person you would disappoint the most if you failed?

What if you free yourself from the fear of letting them down?

For most of us, it is our parents.
We live our life in fear of letting them down.

But we rarely have a conversation with them.
A conversation, to seek permission. To fail.

When the one person we are closest to tells us that they will continue to love us irrespective, we find the courage to face EVERYTHING!

Speak to them today.

And tell them, 'I want to know that you will continue to love and respect me, even if I am in the worst position possible.'

They will never say no!

If you are not having fun while doing it, people will see through it.

You can see it everywhere – the vegetable vendor enjoying their work to the well-paid executive sad as hell in their work.

Happiness (and fun) is a language that communicates through your face and your eyes.

It isn't imposed.
It speaks through who you are.
The one thing that you can never hide.

That is the best part about it. And the worst.

That thing that you still haven't finished and you are mad at yourself for not doing so?
It is simply because it is not a priority.
You think you still have time.

The unfinished art piece isn't a priority for you.
That letter to your mom isn't a priority.
So isn't perhaps cleaning your room.

You think you have the time. However, the only thing you don't have is time!

Priorities get published prima facie.
Procrastination gets promoted to problems.

**Most decisions in life are reversible.
But we assume they are set in stone.**

The second we think decisions are reversible, we start giving serendipity a chance!

We can change most decisions once we make them.
Most of us do not think so, because we attach outcomes to the decisions.

If we start making decisions knowing they are reversible, we will discover how much lies ahead of us just because we decide and act.

Serendipity happens to those who are not married to the outcomes. Instead, to the process.

Knowing when to say no

and saying it

is a life skill.

If you are authentic, if you are truly yourself all the time – you don't have any competition!
No one can ever beat you at being you!

Love to sing? Great! No one, in 'trying to be you while singing' can ever beat you!
You love having a job instead of starting up? No one can ever beat you at enjoying your days at work!

Being yourself in a world that is chasing a yo-yo-ed version of everyone else, is the ultimate reward.
Money, success, worldly pleasures – everything follows the person who chooses to be who they are.
Money, success, worldly pleasures – everything but happiness follows the person who follows inauthenticity to make others happy.

**Merely knowing what you need to do is
not enough for you to do it!
Awareness is the start of the decision.
Not the end of it.**

Step 1 is Awareness.
Step 2 is Execution.
Step 3 is Rinse and Repeat.

You won't go anywhere if you are aware but
don't do anything about it.
You will go everywhere if you are aware and
take actions from that awareness.

You know. You act. You learn. You know
better. And you continue.

It is better to be busy in the chase of finding yourself instead of being busy in the rat race and never know yourself.

Six months back perhaps you were trying your hand at music, along with your day job.
You used to like it back then; however, you were more driven by lyrics.
So now you've become a songwriter for small bands, keeping your day job.

The world may call it a chase.
So be it.

It is still way better than slogging at doing something you hate.
Just because everyone else does the same.

Better to be lost for something worthwhile.
Instead of getting lost in everything worthless.

Comparing yourself to others is the biggest waste of time.

Everyone had different beginnings.
Different temperaments of parents.
Totally different interests and hobbies.
Different ways parents perceived success.
Different teachers who taught you to fit in.

And you expect yourself to outsmart someone else.
It is an insult to your journey. And an insult to what all you have endured to get here.

If you truly want to compare, compare yourself to who you were yesterday.

We always have two choices:

1. **The easy one**
2. **The right one**

It's easy to delay the submission of your work. It's the right thing to submit within timelines. It's easy to gossip about a colleague. It's the right thing to understand their point of view. It's easy to do the easy thing. It's never ever wrong to do the right thing.

You will be rewarded instantly for doing the easy thing.
You will be rewarded eventually for doing the right thing.

We aren't addicted to things.
We are addicted to the emotions that these things generate!

That car, that phone, that social media scrolling, those likes on social media, that brand of clothes, that restaurant, that gimbal, that cuisine – all of these things are what they are: Things.

What we are addicted to, is how these things make us feel.
About ourselves.

It is not the things that are wrong.
It is our inability to understand our emotions.

Don't go to college just looking for a job, a title, a company, a function, a role, a salary.

Go to college looking for yourself.
'What am I good at?'
'What makes me happy?'

The purpose of college is not just education. Education is easily and massively available on the internet.

The purpose of college is to figure out what you enjoy.
The purpose of college is to explore different things, instead of 'settling down.'
The purpose of college is to find yourself!

Take online courses. Pick up internships. Learn how to network. Join online communities. Freelance. Run a startup. Travel solo.

Sit on as many chairs as you can before you find the one chair on which you feel you belong.

If you don't ask, the answer is always no.

144 · DO EPIC SHIT

We always have choices.
No one's ever stuck.
We are just scared to make those choices.

We always know what to do. We are scared of what our best friend might say. We are scared of what our neighbour might gossip. More than anything else, we are scared of failing, or even trying.

So, we stay where we are.

Safe is better than sorry.
Nope.
Risk is better than regret.

Those in your 20s

Look around you.
People are full of regret.
Understand what led to that regret.
That will tell you what not to do.

Those beyond their 20s

Look at you.
You are full of regret.
You know what led to that regret.
Tell others about it, so that they know what not to do.

Do not choose the person you learn from.
Choose what you learn from them.

The most dangerous people in the world are not the ones who are ignorant.

They are the ones who are ignorant but BELIEVE they are right!

You don't control what the world says about you.

You control what YOU say when the world says something about you.

The world is invariably going to talk about you. This shouldn't come as a surprise.

The consequences of those conversations are what you get to decide. You get to control them.

Because how you respond, is how the world will treat you further on.

So, in a way, the way you respond to the world is the way you teach the world how to treat you.

Spent years doing something that you do not enjoy any more?

Think of the time that lies ahead, not of the time that lies in the past!

Whatever has happened, has happened.
For good or for bad, you cannot change it.

But the day you realize what you are doing doesn't work for you any more, you have two options to choose from:

1. Continue with it, because 'I have already spent so much time doing it'
2. Consider what lies ahead

Every single second you continue to hold on to the time gone by is a second away from shaping your future.

The past, however hard-working, shiny and glamorous it was, if it doesn't hold relevance in your present, it makes zero sense to drag it into the future.

People will help you only when you have helped them understand how they can.

The best way to get help is to make it easier for people to help you.
The best way to make it easier for people to help you is by being specific.
The best way to be specific is to reflect upon where exactly you need help. And why?

The distance between 'I could have' and 'I have' is regret.

I could have continued with my PhD in the US, done well in it, despite the fact that it did not make me happy.

OR

I dropped my PhD, came back to India, didn't know what to do next, took up a job at Rs 15,000 per month, and joined a five-year-old business school taking a loan of Rs 14 lakh.

But what I did get was the self-comfort of abandoning the comfort zone, and going after a decision just because I felt it might make me happy. And it did!

What I didn't want to answer was the question, 'What if you had dropped out of your PhD because it didn't make you happy, and instead explored what could make you happy?'

What I didn't want to answer was the question, 'What if?'

The hardest thing in the world is telling yourself that it's not hard at all.

It is not hard to wake up early.
It is not hard to make money.
It is not hard to approach strangers.
It is not hard to express love.
It is not hard to send cold emails.
It is not hard to ask for a raise.
It is not hard to ask questions.
It is not hard to voice your opinion.

What's hard is convincing your mind that it is not hard.
That you can do it.

If you are scared of losing
You have already lost!

Loss is a result.
Fear is an input.

You don't control your results.
You always control your inputs.

If you don't try because you are scared of losing, you have put in motion the input of losing.

Once you have decided your input, you have already created your output. Of losing.

The most memorable moments of your life would have a sense of freedom attached to them.

That moment of passing your exams, because now you would be financially independent!
Those moments of awe in meditation, when you figured it was possible to break your inner patterns!
The moment of simply getting out of the city on your car or bike.

We remember the moments not for what they are.
We remember the moments for what they make us feel.

We remember the moments not for where they take place.
We remember the moments for where they take us within.

Instead of worrying about what might happen, anticipate what might happen.

Our power to imagine is both a strength and a weakness.

We may imagine what if we fail in our dream project.
Or we may imagine what if our dream project takes off with flying colours.

We can build our own prisons through our thoughts, or let go of all bars, break ceilings and imagine the best outcome possible.

Stack by stack.
Moment by moment.
Story by story.

Our power to imagine comes to haunt us. Or help us.
The one we pick. Is the one we live with.

Life is full of struggle.

There will be a struggle in trying to live with the world by its rules.

And there will be a struggle in trying to build your own world and your own rules.

You get to choose your struggle.

. . .

A corporate job can be a great start to a career.

1. Teaches you the value of structure, processes and systems.
2. Teaches you how small individual actions come together to form a bigger whole.
3. Gives you stability early on.

You do not become cool by shitting on corporate jobs.

. . .

Do not mistake starting slow as starting small.

. . .

You are not the only one confused.
You are not the only one unsure.
You are not the only one struggling.
You are not dumb, inadequate, incapable.

Everyone is struggling.
Everyone is figuring it out.

Don't be harsh on yourself.

. . .

When it comes to money, more information doesn't make people more aware.
It makes them more scared.

. . .

Being grateful in life for what you have is precious.

As adults, the single biggest hurdle to learning is pride!

I'm a grown-up now. I know everything!

Most adults repeat this to themselves in some shape and form, thus living in a prison.

It's okay to not know!
It's okay to accept things you don't know!!
It's more than okay to learn even after you've become an adult!!!

Because those who learn, irrespective of their age, are the ones who continue to grow.

The greatest illusion is that life should be perfect!

People who are enjoying their lives are at a competitive advantage.

Imagine having all the money you want and being miserable!
Imagine living life on your own terms and enjoying it like no one else :)

Joy is the ultimate advantage. Everything else just follows.

If you didn't say it earlier, don't say it during your exit interview.

Instead of giving vent to your anger at the time of leaving the company, it always helps to have a conversation with your management when you are a part of it.

The best companies get built by candid conversations, instead of irreversible irritations at the time of your exit.

A meaningful job need not be one that completely consumes your whole life.

You may love your job.
And find impeccable joy in it.
Yet if it leaves you with zero or little space for yourself, it is not the one!

It's important to have your space.
It's super important to not let your job encroach upon your life.
And it is respectful of yourself to respect those boundaries.

To find meaning in your job is beautiful. Your job being the only meaning of life is scary.

To not have a plan and be okay with it is the best plan. It will take everything to get to that point.

We are all told, 'you gotta have a plan'.
If Plan A doesn't work, then Plan B.
If Plan B doesn't work, then Plan C.
So on and so forth.
'Always gotta have a plan.'

However, imagine yourself being asked, 'Where do you see yourself five years from now?' and you reply,
'I do not know.
And I am OK with that.'

THAT right there is liberating.
It is freedom.
That is being at peace with where you are in life, with who you are in life.

If you are comfortable dancing in public without alcohol or drugs, you are at peace with who you are.

If you feel high without being high,
If you are intoxicated by joy instead of substances,
If you love to express yourself without numbing your senses,
You are at a place of untouchable joy and peace.

The only intake you need is more self-belief that you are just perfect as you are!

The easiest way to learn from mistakes is to read books.
The next option is to commit them yourself.

Books are a great way to learn from mistakes someone else has made over their lifetime!

Why would you want to commit them again?

If given a choice between a Rs 300 book plus a couple of hours reading it or 10 years of making mistakes, what would you choose?

You can get anything back in life but not time. And the best way to collapse the timeline is by deriving lessons from others' timelines and making them your own.

Resisting the obvious is a great way to change your orbit. If you do what everyone else will do, you will end up like everyone else.

Here's how I resist the obvious.

While making a decision, I ask myself, 'What would most people do?'

Then I consider alternate options.

This one question has led to so many opportunities and different directions than I could have imagined had I opted for the obvious route.

Only when you go against the flow will you find your own flow.

Complaining has never ever led someone to a solution.

Complaining amplifies the problem.
It justifies why it exists.
Makes us feel the victim, the person subject to the miseries created by the problem.

All of this robs you of your power. And tricks you into believing that you don't have any.

If you had to choose just one habit for the rest of your life, let it be of not complaining. And see how effortlessly you reach solutions.

The real problem was never the real problem.
The real problem was the compound interest of complaining.

Working out teaches you discipline and patience like few other things do.

You can't buy a fit body.
You can't get fit overnight.
You can't cheat to get to a fit body.
You can't ride on someone else to get a fit body.
You can't blame anybody for not being fit.
Neither can you ask someone to get fit on your behalf.

It is only going to happen if you show up every day.
And be patient.

And that's a valuable lesson.
For life!

The most dangerous
people are those
who run away from
change.

They are also the most
energy sucking.

Don't ever fool yourself to believe you deserve to be where you are in life.

Entitlement is a trap.
It makes us look into the mirror and believe we have worked hard to be where we are. That we deserve it.

The truth is, we don't deserve it. We are just plain lucky.
Lucky that we were born and raised in a family that gave us love, food, care, shelter, education, value. An upbringing.

Because of which we sit on opportunities that we take for granted.
And few outside of our world will get to experience even for a second of their lives.
They work far harder than we ever will.
Are most likely smarter than we are.

Gratitude. Not entitlement.

How you treat
someone who has
nothing to offer
defines your value
system.

Your values don't help
you grow.

But in times of
shit, they hold you
together.

You will get what you seek.
Not what you desire.
Not what you dream.

What you seek. Fervently.

Do you seek validation? Or do you seek contentment?
Do you seek money and loneliness? Or do you seek money and happiness?
Do you seek social status? Or do you wish to be not known for what you do?

We may show to the world that we seek something different from what we truly seek. Yet hand on heart, we always know what we truly seek.

And the universe has a beautiful system of landing what you ask for, on your plate.

The question is, are we seeking things that make us seek even more or seek less?

PART 4

ENTREPRENEURSHIP

I have been an entrepreneur on paper since 2009.

I have been an informal entrepreneur though since the age of 11, when my friends and I started a comic-renting 'startup' out of a mat (called as 'chaarpai' in Indian households).

We made Rs 11 the first day :)

Along the years, I have learnt a great deal.

Mostly through my mistakes.

Reflecting on those mistakes and failures has helped me grow, much more than any success has.

Here are my reflections, stemming from my love for entrepreneurship even before I knew how to pronounce it correctly.

As a founder, if you won't show up every single day, despite how you are feeling or how the startup is doing or what the press is writing about you or your co-founders not working out or your product failing or your customers shouting,

No one is going to do it for you.

. . .

People would much rather work for a competent asshole than an incompetent nice guy.

. . .

Entrepreneurship is f**king hard.

The early excitement of building a team, planning a name, launching the first version will fade away.

And insane details that life has, will begin to emerge.
At that point, there is only one thing that will help.

The stories you tell yourself.
Keep reminding yourself of why you became a founder in the first place.
You wanted to be happy doing it, feel fulfilled being one, or desired peace from it.
Or whatever else it was.
Because that is the only thing that matters.

Capability is rarely the question mark in life.

It is always the intent.

No one lacks talent. People are best at what they do. Or they know how to figure it out.

What people lack is intent.

Lack of intent because they don't like the leader.
Lack of intent because they are not driven.
Lack of intent because they don't care.
Lack of intent because they are not acknowledged.
Lack of intent because they work for a person not for a larger good.

When people are driven to bring their right intent to the table, they are the first ones to surprise themselves with their capabilities.

Telling someone they are wrong is never going to convince the person.

Telling someone they don't see the point is hypocritical.

Telling someone you will never understand is you facing the mirror.

Yes, people do go wrong.
They do not see the point.
Yes, they do not even understand.

None of this is false.

However, entrepreneurship and building a team is ninety per cent understanding and ten per cent execution.
Ninety per cent empathy with ten per cent autocracy.
And hundred per cent patience.

'If I can't trust you, it doesn't matter how smart you are.'

The best advice I have ever got!

My first manager told me this.
After he used to detect errors in my work consistently.
I used to think it was my manager's work to detect my errors.
Wrong!

It was my job to deliver error-free work. It was my manager's job to build upon that.
I was failing at my basic job, instead of growing at it.

Your work is not only your work. It is the measure of how much trust your manager places in you. Dip by dip. Day by day. One action at a time.

Entrepreneurship is not a profession.

It's a state of mind.

You can have a job and think of building new things, energizing your team and making sure you are helping the business grow.

Figure out the right problems to solve. Ask for work beyond your job description. Treat your job like your own business.

You do not necessarily need to have a start-up in order to become an entrepreneur.

You can start where you are. Move things that need to be moved. Change the status quo for the better. And you are an entrepreneur.

Compounding is the biggest miracle of life.
Founder dilution also is, in a bad way.

For the longest time, you would continue investing religiously, you would see normal gains. Over time, the gains would sky rocket.

So is the case with founder dilution. When your startup is small, you don't feel you're giving away much, while inviting external funding.

It is only when the company creates big results, that you as a founder realize that much of your large profits and valuation also get split in a big way. Compounding, in a way you hadn't wanted yet signed up for.

When was the last time you bought a product or service, because the founder is from IIT or because the founder hasn't drawn a salary for the past six months or because the founder is going through depression?

You couldn't care less! No one cares a f**k about who you are.

What you have done in the past does not have any relevance to how good you are at solving customer problems.

Your success as a founder depend on how close you are able to get people to their solutions.

Who you are and where you came from doesn't matter.
What you do and where you are going, is all that does.

The market doesn't care about titles.
The market (rightly) only cares about its tantrums.

Congratulating an entrepreneur on raising funds is like congratulating a chef on buying vegetables.

Money is the ingredient to the startup recipe.
It is the start. Not end.

Acknowledge the milestone.
Wish them well.
Share your faith in them.
But don't make them believe they have won.
Don't believe you have won, if you raise funds.

No one has won.
Not as yet.

'I trust you not because you know everything. I trust you because I know that you will do everything in your capacity to find the answer.'

This is what I tell my most capable team members.

No one knows all the answers.

However, the best players that move the needle forward, know how to figure out solutions to complex problems.

You don't become the most capable one when you know the answers.
You become the most capable one when you go beyond 'I don't know'.
And surprise everyone in the process. Including yourself.

Attitude >> Experience >> Education

The hiring principle I have always followed.

Skills can be taught.
Attitude is really hard to teach.

While finding the right people for your team, it always helps to pick the ones who embody the culture of your team.

Even if they lack the skills, their attitude will help them grow.

An optimistic, driven individual will figure out a way to learn more.
A successful skilled individual will struggle hard to grow if they see pessimism in every possibility.

Attitude compensates for skills.
Skills never compensate for attitude.

When I asked my first boss, how come there was always this unequal distribution of work even within the same team, he replied,

'Good people pay a far higher price for being good than bad people pay for being bad.'

He wasn't talking about work.
He was talking about life.

Build a team so strong that someone from outside doesn't know who the boss is!

Do you admit your mistakes?
Do you allow your team to make mistakes?
Do you trust your team members to do their work?
Do you ask questions instead of offering prescriptions?
Do you give them autonomy instead of micromanaging the team?

If this is how you run your team, no one from the outside would be able to guess who leads it. Because now, everyone is a leader!

Entrepreneurship is the most brutal way to discover yourself.

There are initial days of fun of a new office, pristine furniture, and branding.
Then come the finer details.
Making money.
Building a team.
Growing fast.
Developing a culture.

How you handle yourself and your mental state during the times when everything is not a bed of roses, truly determines who you are.

It definitely won't be as easy or glamorous as you had expected. However, it will reveal so much to you about yourself, that you won't wish the journey was different in any way.

Fortunately, or unfortunately, nothing shows you who you are as much as entrepreneurship does.

The toughest skill as a leader is to be calm during the toughest moments.

Anyone can be calm when you are hitting numbers or when a customer is satisfied.

The power to be calm when your team's morale is low, the power to empower your team members despite their mistakes, and the drive to move them forward when things aren't moving forward are the greatest skills.

It isn't easy. That is why leadership is a reflection of who you are.

Tough.
But a lot easier than losing your temper.

With leadership comes the power to lose your calm.
Leaders who don't lose it are truly powerful.

Show people who they can be.
Instead of telling them who they shouldn't be.

One the best lessons I learnt as a people manager.

'You shouldn't pull others down, be disrespectful of others or make fun of someone's mental health issues.'
Stating this is being preachy.
It's the truth, but it is simply moral science.
Everyone knows it.

What if you are the one who shows people their potential.
What if you could show people that it is so empowering to respect others for who they are?
What if you do everything you want your team to embody?

Words are wise.
However, stories strike.

Most people who want to start a business think they should quit their job and start a startup.

Not true, in my opinion.

Work nights/weekends and test your idea out.

The minute you HAVE to push the startup and work to make money, it is very different from 'let's see if this even works.'

Irrational optimism is a founder's death trap!

. . .

The hardest moment while building a startup is when you let down your team.

The most precious moment while building a startup is when you let down your team and they are the ones who pick you up.

Build a culture that picks people up when they are down.

Be a part of such a culture.

When you raise money, it is not an achievement.

It is an obligation.

When you raise money, you are no longer answerable only to customers.
You are answerable to investors because they desire a return.
Because they have raised money from someone who is also looking for a return.

You are not focusing on growing the business now.
You are under the pressure of growing the business.

And that's a huge obligation!

Sorry to break your heart . . .

Somebody out there has ALREADY come up with the same idea that you have! Somebody out there is ALREADY working on the same idea that you have!

Don't overindex on the idea.
Instead, find out what it is that they know that you don't.

Ideas are hardly new.

What's new is solving an unsolved problem in an existing idea.
For that, you first need to learn what it is that others before you already know, that you don't know as yet.

Your idea is not your startup.
Your approach is your startup.

The worst thing a company does to its employees is:

1. **Rate them once a year**
2. **Tell them how well they did**
3. **Measure them on metrics they didn't even know they were being assessed on**

It's sad that most employees do not know for the entire twelve months what the management is thinking about them!

The best feedback is:
- stated in real time/fortnightly/weekly
- being candid instead of springing a surprise
- being helpful instead of an FYI

It is the employees that run the company, not the other way around.

- The moment companies become aware of this truth, everything changes!

Asshole founders don't build institutions.

They merely start and run companies.

It is easy for anyone to start a company.
It is super difficult to build a place where people would love to come to work, where people are respected for who they are, and most importantly, where people grow at work and as individuals.

Anyone can start and run a company.
To be so poor that all they have is money.

The real game is to have conversations with every team member.
To listen to them just with the intent of listening to them.
To know them, because that is what will help you make wiser decisions.

Only courageous founders go beyond themselves and run institutions.

The three worst reasons to become an entrepreneur:

1. **I want to make money**
2. **I hate my current job**
3. **Everyone is doing it**

Entrepreneurship is hard.

For the longest time it won't give you the luxuries of a salaried job.

Also, you will have multiple bosses instead of one.

Most people fail as entrepreneurs because they pick one of these external reasons to become entrepreneurs.

Only when your drive is internal, you are curious, you are consumed by a problem, you would be able to experience the joy of becoming an entrepreneur.

You want to solve a problem and while you hope for success, you are ready for failure too.

A great leader should be replaceable when it comes to their tasks and actions.

And irreplaceable when it comes to their thoughts and vision.

Great leaders are those who make themselves dispensable over time.
Because they don't care about feeding their ego.

The best leader allows their team to execute in their absence.
While the leader works to define the purpose and end goal.

In a society where being trusted is not common, operating with trust is a competitive advantage.
People inherently want to be trusted.

I pay my team (interns as well as full-time) on the first day of every month.
Also, I trust them on Day 1 instead of building it over time.

When people are trusted, especially in a trust-deficient context, you get more out of them.

People want to be trusted. They just aren't given enough opportunities to.
And once they are trusted, they not only surprise you, they also end up surprising themselves by the accountability they deliver!

PART 5
MONEY

When I was young, my father shared an interesting side of money with me.

He said, because you grew up without money, you would either go after money or you would grow beyond money.

While I always think money is important, it is the worst use of your time and life to keep running after it.

Money buys freedom.

Freedom is a privilege.

That freedom helps you make wiser choices.

However, before those wiser choices, I have made several mistakes with money.

I share them with you in the hope that you are aware of them and make a meaningful relationship with money.

Mistakes I made with money

We grew up without any money.
Perpetually in debt. Hand-to-mouth existence.
Which is why I grew up hating money.
I thought it was the cause of all our problems.
And I never wanted money to rule over me.

What I didn't realize though was that this desire to dismiss money led me to disrespect it.

Because I had a knack of making money, I never really spent any effort in understanding how to manage and grow it.

In the process, I ended up making a lot of mistakes.

Mistake 1
I took loans to buy real estate.
Assuming the price appreciation would take care of the interest rate I pay.
I didn't take into account taxes.

I didn't take into account inflation.

I didn't do the maths, that to get a respectable return, the price will have to grow approximately twenty per cent year-on-year.

Mistake 2

Whenever I made any extra cash, instead of paying off the loan, I invested it in startups. Convinced that the startup would multiply my money several times over.

I basically went to a casino convinced I would make enough money to repay my loans.

That's what I did!

Mistake 3

I invested in illiquid assets – startups, real estate.
And rarely in liquid assets – stocks, gold.

So, when tough times happened, I had a lot of 'paper wealth' but no cash.

Which meant collecting even more debt.
Never trying to pay it back.

Because hey, the previous example – of not paying off loans with extra cash!

Mistake 4
For an entire decade I took lower-than-market salary, overindexing on equity.
I believed the equity would make me much more than the salary ever would.
So when things didn't end up as expected, I was left with no wealth.

Mistake 5
I overindexed on the future.
Continued to maintain my lifestyle when I should have lowered it.
Maxed my credit cards.
Accumulated more debt.

All in the hope that one mega event in the future would resolve all issues.

Mistake 6

I invested in stocks when the markets went high, in the hope of making fast money.
I sold in panic when the market tanked, so that I didn't lose money.

It should have been the exact opposite.

Mistake 7

Whenever I was in need of money, I broke my mutual fund investment to generate cash.

I basically broke compounding.
I persisted with it during the painful slow-growth period.
And just when compounded growth was about to take off, I clipped its wings.

Mistake 8

I discouraged my wife from investing in mutual funds and buying gold.
She still did.
I mocked her, laughed at her.

Challenged her to a return comparison at the end of the decade.

It was her investment that saved us.
Not once, thrice.

Because I hated money, I never respected it.
And I realized that money didn't respect me either.

While I knew how to make it, I never understood how to preserve it.
How to grow it.

Today I think I know.

1. Taxes are a thing. A real thing.
   Always look at your tax-adjusted returns when comparing.

2. Inflation is a thing. A real thing.
   Money loses value over time. Always include that in your return calculation.

3. Compounding rests on a very important element – time. You need time to witness compounding in action. Give it time. A lot of time.

4 Liquidity is critical. Invest in a way that you can withdraw cash whenever you need. Else what's the point?

5. If you have excess cash, wait.
   Wait for the right opportunity.
   Wait patiently.
   Wait for markets to drop.

   Wait.
   The price you buy at, determines your return.

   'No one wants to get rich slowly.'
                                   – Warren Buffet

6. When in your 20s, live like a pauper.
   Live within your means.

Pay your bills, and then pay yourself by
investing.
Pay for your desires last.
Do not take loans for your desires.

7. Take loans only for things that appreciate
   in value.
   Education.
   Maybe a house. Only one!

8. Do not invest according to your echo
   chamber.

   Angel invest because you are a founder.
   Invest in stocks because you are in finance.
   Invest in gold because you are a trader.
   Get to learn and respect all asset classes.

9. Double down on what is working rather
   than diversify. Diversification will not yield
   supernormal returns.
   Owning more of what is working, will.

10. Allow compounding to happen.

    It takes time. Decades.

    For the longest time it will seem nothing is happening.

    It is happening!

The biggest lesson that I have learnt about money is that it buys you freedom.

And freedom is a privilege.

For the longest time I denied myself this freedom.

And today when I do have it, I realized all the mistakes I made that prevented me from getting this freedom.

These mistakes have made me wise today.

I hope they make you wise today, much earlier!

10 common money mistakes to avoid

Mistake 1
Not valuing your time and treating it like its free.

We don't know how much our one hour costs.
We don't know how much we ACTUALLY spend when we watch Netflix two hours a day.
We don't know how much we should charge for a project.

We don't understand how our time equals money.

Mistake 2
Spending your time on things that are easy to measure money-wise.

We will spend half a day travelling to one end of the city to save Rs 1000, because we know we will conclusively save that amount.

But we won't spend two hours preparing for our salary negotiation!

Mistake 3

Taking too many loans.

We overindex on our future earnings.
And spend more today than we can afford.

Loans tie us down.
They increase our burn rate.
They make us risk-averse.
They make us feel like we are stuck!

Mistake 4

Believing that our income is capped.

Our income is not capped. There is no upper limit to how much we can earn.
Instead, it is our spending that is capped. We have to spend a bare minimum to live, to survive.

Instead of reducing expenses, focus on increasing income.

Mistake 5
Trying to time the market.

Market is too high. Let it fall.
Market is low. Right time to buy.

No one knows the highs or lows of a market.
The best way to invest over a long term is to invest regularly. Irrespective of the price at that time.

Mistake 6
Investing because of FOMO.

Everyone is investing in Bitcoin. I should too.
Everyone is selling Bitcoin. I should too.
Everyone is buying ITC. I should too.
Everyone is selling ITC. I should too.

Everyone is NOT you!
Invest in your beliefs and research and as per your appetite.

Mistake 7
Renting your time and not owning any assets.

Everyone in a job isn't going to create supernormal wealth.
Because we have to spend time working, to earn.

Assets, on the other hand, make money, even when we sleep.
Start a company. Own stocks. Create rental income.

Mistake 8
Investing late.

20s is the time to have fun. Will start investing in the 30s.
30s is the time to build a family and enjoy it. Will start investing in the 40s.

The right time to start investing was when you turned 18.
The next best time is TODAY.

Mistake 9
Comparing your money to others.

Money, for most of us, is an outcome. Not an input.
It is the result of the decisions we have made, not the reason for the decisions we made.

Compare the decisions people made to get to money.
Comparing the outcome won't help!

Mistake 10
Running after money.
Money gives you freedom.
Freedom is a privilege.

But the minute we run after money we are not free any more.

Use money to earn your freedom.
Don't give up your freedom to earn money.

Bonus
Not taking risks, when you can.

In our 20s, when we have little to lose. And even if we do lose, we have time to recover.
Lesser so in our 30s/40s.
That's why our parents love fixed deposits.
But we shouldn't.

Take risks early on.
And don't worry about the short-term ups and downs.

I wish money was a topic that our parents spoke about, or our schools/colleges did justice to.

In the absence of it, we are left to learn from those who have made mistakes and realized what to do.

Or make those same mistakes ourselves.

Three books that have helped me tremendously to understand money:

- Rich Dad Poor Dad
- Psychology of Money
- Intelligent Investor

Three people who have taught me a lot about money:

- Ruchi, my wife
- Naval Ravikant
- Morgan Housel

If you do not know how to care for money, money will stay away from you.

— Robert Kiyosaki

10 lies I was told about money

Lie 1
Money is the root cause of all evil.

From an early age, thinking about money was not encouraged.
It was the unsaid rule that money is important, but thinking about it is evil.
After all, money was the reason behind fights, wars, disagreements.

Now I know, it is not money that is the cause.
It is the importance we attach to it in our lives.

Money is simply a medium of transaction.
When it becomes an emotion, that is when it consumes us.

And that is true for all things in life!

Lie 2

Be wary of those who are rich.

It was always assumed that getting rich was possible only through exploitation of others, being cold-blooded and twisting the law in your favour.

The rich are the ones who have compromised on their morals.

Now I know that for every immoral rich person, there are countless more examples of people who treat money, people and values with respect.

It's just that, by design, they are not the ones we hear of or speak of.
News covers the abnormal. Not the normal.

Lie 3
Saving money is important.

Of course saving is important. But we were never told the complete story.
That investing is more important.

Post demonetization, all the money 'saved' by our parents came out. They were lauded for their saving capabilities.
Most 'savings' approaches that we were taught destroy the value of money.

To make your money beat inflation, we were never taught how to invest.

Lie 4
Buying jewellery is an investment.

We bought jewellery at the smallest excuse. It not only added to the social status, it was also considered a wise choice because gold appreciated in value over time.

It was an investment.

Now I know, gold is an investment, jewellery is not.

When we disguise our desires as our needs, we almost always end up making a mistake.

Lie 5
Buying a house is the ultimate financial goal.

Paying rent was the classic middle-class curse. And also, the middle-class crime towards oneself.

Our own home, as early as we can buy one, gives us the security we deserve and the status we ought to have.

Now I know buying a house early in your life is binding and thus can be a regret-filled decision.

It most likely doesn't make financial sense (do the maths), it also binds you to a size, to a city and to a locality that you will always find hard to escape.

Lie 6
All expensive things that we buy are assets.

The way to define an asset was by 'how expensive it is'. The more the cost, the better the asset.
Started with home appliances, then scooter, then car, then house.
Buying 'assets' was the middle-class indulgence!

Now I know most of these are not assets. Even the house we stay in.

The only two assets that I perhaps built over years was my network and my content.
None of which I had to pay for, with money.
It was bought through my time.

Lie 7
Taking loans and using credit cards is a sign of your confidence in your future.

Because you believe in yourself, you can afford something now, as against in the future.
And the fact that someone approved that loan, or made you eligible for it, is testimony to that fact.

Now I know.

Financially smart people take loans even if they can afford, to save money.
Financially weak people take loans knowing that they can't afford, to spend money!

Lie 8
There are two ways to get rich – either work in the same place for a really long time or keep changing jobs every one to two years!

Getting rich was either pegged to your

provident fund and gratuity amount or to the 'jump' that you got if you changed jobs.

Now I know that your salary has nothing to do with your wealth.
It is not how much you earn in a job that determines your net worth.
It is how much do you own of what makes money for you, even when you are sleeping.

Lie 9
The only way to make money is to get an education.

You go to college, get a job, start saving, buy a house, keep doing well in your job, keep getting a raise.
And you are rich.

That is the path.
The predictable path.
The only path!

The financially wisest people I know are not just the ones who followed this path, but also the ones who followed no path.

They kept creating/buying assets – whether their own company, whether stocks, whether intellectual property, whether a side gig, whether investing.

They didn't settle with where they were.

Lie 10
Once you get rich, give money to those who do not have it.

Giving money is a noble action.
And when you have the means to, you should help others.
That brings good karma, brings you more money, and thus makes you give more.

The circle continues.

Now I know, it is not money that makes people change their orbit. It is an opportunity.
I spend my money helping others not by giving them money, but instead by creating opportunities.
So that tomorrow they might not need my money.

Growing up . . .

Dreaming of earning a lot of money was a taboo, investing money was never discussed and spending money was always considered a socially desirable action.

Worst was that no one knew that they were believing in lies.
My parents, my relatives, my network genuinely believed all these lies to be true.

They guided me and influenced me with the best intentions.
Just that they weren't the right ones.

It took a lot of mistakes, a lot of undoing and a lot of reflection to get to a point where I began to see the truth for what it was worth.

My hope for all of you is that you get there much before me.

PART 6
RELATIONSHIPS

Relationships are the place where we thrive.

They are also the place where we are challenged the most.

One of my favourite books, *The Courage to be Disliked* states that all problems are interpersonal relationship problems.

I'd not disagree.

And, it all begins with having the right relationship with the most important person: YOU.

Hope these reflections of mine help you, as much as they help me as well:

Would you be friends with your own self?
Would you marry yourself?
Would you be your own boss?
What version of you would you rather not be?

Why do you still continue being that version?

There are some flaws in you that you would never like to see in anyone else.

Yet you keep living with those flaws.
If something is unacceptable to you in others, it must be something that must be unacceptable to you in yourself in the first place.

The change we want in others is the change we need to begin with.

We invite what we allow.

You can neither choose your parents nor what they end up doing to you psychologically. Be prepared to heal yourself, if you have to.

The only thing we do not choose is the family we are born to.
The only thing that has the maximum impact on us as kids is the family we are born to.

This may be good news for some. And tragedy for others.

Most people choose to live with this tragedy. And call it fate.
The bold ones choose to change what happened to them by actively healing themselves.

What's stopping you from making the bold choice?
Healing isn't an option. It is a necessity.

Holding a grudge against someone requires a lot of effort.
Think of all the wasted time spent being mad at someone.

Someone broke you into pieces. And now you have decided to trade your peace for seeking revenge.

When we hold a grudge against someone, we do the same thing they did to us: hurt us. They hurt us once. We hurt ourselves 100x by repeating it in our head.

Every problem in this world can be traced back to a point of miscommunication.

All relationships thrive on communication.

Feeling upset with someone? Why not talk? Feeling upset with yourself? Why not talk to yourself?

Once we know how to communicate and we do communicate, problems move from being problems to actions to be taken.

There is a big difference between saying thank you and feeling thankful.

Saying 'thank you' to please someone. Or saying 'thank you' because you were truly grateful.

One shows obligation. The other shows admiration.

We create our relationships by what we choose to give.

Nothing teaches you better than teaching others.

When you learn anything, you make it a part of you.
When you teach anything, you make it a part of others.

To make others understand things, you simplify them further.
Break down what you already know.
Through which you create your own breakthroughs.

To start with 'you're right' is great.

To do so in public, when you don't have to is greatness!

Your kindness might cause you pain, a sense of betrayal, heartburn. Be kind anyway.

Not everyone is going to reciprocate your kindness.
Some are even going to play with it.
Some are not going to care.
Some are not going to acknowledge it ever.

Yet, kindness is always the right thing to do.

Not for anyone's validation.
For your own.

Because who would you be, if you are not kind?

Unpopular opinion:

Empathy cannot be taught. You are either born with it or not.

Empathy = I understand what you are going through.

From so many years of meeting and interacting with people, here is what I know for sure:

Empathy is either your innate quality or it isn't.
No one can teach you to understand others.
No one can teach you to put yourself in others' shoes.

You either have it. Or you don't. There is no work-in-progress.

When you realize the truth of this statement, you get to decide who is worth spending your time on, who is your tribe, and whom to say no to.

Sympathy: I feel sorry for you.
Empathy: I can understand what you must be going through.
Respect: I admire the way you are handling this.

Respect >> Empathy >> Sympathy

Sympathy is a form of pity.

Empathy is rising above it and thinking at par with someone who is going through.

Respect is rising beyond what they are going through, and letting them know that they are doing a beautiful job.

No one is useless.

Everyone knows something you don't.

When we approach people with the mindset that they don't know anything, we close all doors to learning something new.

Only when we shut the door of our ego and be open to learning something new do we realize how much we don't know!

Everyone has stories.
Stories that create their filters.
Filters that create their stains or clean them.

And almost every story, comes with a knowledge that you don't have.
That isn't surprising, rather relieving.

Knowing that you don't know much, is the best knowledge!

By not appreciating someone for their vulnerability and truth, all we do is encourage lying.

Remember the time you did something wrong as a kid?
And instead of lying, you decided to own up and tell your parents about it?

However, you got scolded, instead of being appreciated for speaking the truth.
That becomes your worldview. That is how you figure how the world works.

Are we doing the exact same thing with people around us?

And subconsciously telling them that speaking the truth is not an act of courage?

Truth, as scary and scarry as it is, comes with the courage to speak up. And stand by it.

True respect is when you respect someone even after you've got to know them.

It's easy to respect someone online or from a distance. But that isn't respect. It's infatuation.

It's hard to replicate that respect when you know them beyond the perceived persona.

Now they're not acting.
They are without their mask.
Bare and barren.

That is when your admiration turns into either loathing or respect.

Run away from those who are trying to run away from themselves.

Those who are not willing to heal themselves.
Those who do not want to know their deeper parts.
Those who are not okay and do nothing to change it.
Those who do not want to have difficult conversations with themselves.

Run away from those who never run towards themselves.

Do not show up for every argument you are invited to!

An undeniable life hack for your peace.

The nature of arguments is that they thrive on more inputs.
If your only input in every argument is your silence, peace follows naturally.

Respect doesn't come from the title.

It comes from conduct.

Respect doesn't come if you are a CEO, founder, leader, manager, or senior.
Respect comes from what you do and who you are.

And you don't need any title to get there.
What you do becomes your title.
How you treat others is your business card.

There are people who tell you that you are wrong.
There are people that help you see where you are wrong.

Guess which ones are more important?

The ones who tell you that you're wrong are the ones imposing their beliefs on you.

The ones who help you see where you are wrong are the ones encouraging you to form your own beliefs.

Some impose. Others show.
Some poke. Others make you more awake.
Some show you how you are wrong. Others teach you how to be right.

It takes effort to find love.

It takes effort to feel fulfilled.

It takes effort to be fit.

It takes effort to be happy.

Which is why most of us do not have love, fulfilment, happiness or fitness in our life.

. . .

We all accept the love we think we deserve.

Love is contingent.

Not on the ones loving us.
Rather on our definition of love.
And how much we love ourselves.

If we think we are not worthy of love, we will subconsciously deny it.
If we truly believe we are worthy of love, we will take the smallest compliments with grace and ease.

People who are loved the most, are the ones who BELIEVE that they are worthy of love.

We don't have to agree with each other as long as we understand each other.

The best relationship doesn't necessarily agree on everything.

The best relationships have the best acceptance despite their differences.

When we want only our say in relationships, we miss out on the bigger picture.
When we respect our differences, we love people for who they truly are.

Who you decide to spend your life with. One of the biggest decisions you will make in your life.

Don't take it lightly.

The partner you pick will directly or indirectly decide your free time, work, finances and most importantly, your happiness.

This is the one decision that could be painful to reverse.
This is the one decision that will influence almost all your decisions.
This is the one decision that will either make you feel proud or suffocated every morning.

Your parents are first humans. Then parents.

Which means they too can be wrong.

They too can be toxic.

They too can be unreasonable.

Do not think they are above all of this.

As long as you are financially dependent on your parents, you are answerable to them.

If you wish to be independent of them, while still respecting them as your parents, buy yourself financial freedom.

Whenever someone says 'You will never know how I am feeling', remind yourself that they are telling you life's most fundamental truth.

We will never know!
We will never truly understand what the other person is going through.

This might hurt, especially if you love them dearly.

However, true love sometimes means understanding that you don't understand.

Your true friends are those who are TRULY happy for you when you succeed.

Be that true friend for others.

Most people say true friends are the ones who are there for us in our tough times.
I believe that's wrong.

Anyone can be there for us in our tough times. What we truly want to have are friends who are never jealous of what we have achieved, rather celebrate us for that!

However, it is rare to find such friends.

Most either gossip in private groups, or are never truly happy.

But we all wish we had one.
What if we became that one?
When you give what you desire the most, you don't desire it any more.

If you share because you are expecting something in return, it is not sharing.

It is a transaction!

Wanting to maintain a distance from someone you do not relate to any more doesn't mean you don't care about them.

It just means you care about the relationship you have with yourself more than the one you have with them.

We change courses.
Some don't.

We learn to let go.
Some don't.

We grow more positive.
Some don't.

It's okay to not relate to them any more.
It's okay to be emotionally away.
It's okay to respect your growth while they don't respect theirs.

It doesn't mean you don't care.
It means you cannot care about anyone unless you care about yourself.

Stay away from relationships that suck energy out of you.

These relationships are rarely give and take.

They only take. And you have only so much to give.

How we treat others is a reflection of how we treat ourselves.

It is rare, almost impossible, for a mean, conniving, hurtful, racist, bigoted person to truly love themselves.

We bring people down because we are feeling low.
We make fun of them because we are not in a self-respecting place in our lives.
We don't think twice before hurting others because we are hurt deeply.

We may not want to admit that.
People who are truly pierced within are rarely seen having inner peace.

However, truly happy, fulfilled and soaring people never ever make others feel bad about themselves.

The inner world drives the outer. Period.

We are not the average of the five people we spend the most time with.

We are the average of the five thoughts we spend the most time with.

And those thoughts needn't come from people in our life.

Our thoughts come from people we follow on social media, the books, podcasts, anything we consume.

We aren't with people any more.

We are with ideas, thoughts and identities. Pick wisely.

Lessons I learnt from my parents

Papa joined a young company as a sales representative. Within a year, he got a call from another company. 2x salary plus a car. This was 1985. And a big deal.

He took the offer.

Two years down, the company shuts.
The company he quit, Ranbaxy, becomes a giant.

Dad was jobless for a year . . .

I remember sitting as a family, filling ballpen refills because he was paid for every 100 pens filled.
I remember days when Ma and Papa had just one meal a day.

But my sister and I went to the best schools possible.

We knew we didn't have money, but were never made to feel so.

Papa took a risk. And it didn't pay off.
He could never recover from it.
But he would take the same risk again if he had to.

Lesson:
Risk and failure are a state of mind.
There should never be any fear.
And no regret.

Ma is one of the most empathetic people I know.

Her sensitivity is her super power, because she has a knack for knowing what the other person might be feeling.

Whenever there was a conflict in my head or I was angry at someone, she always used to ask, 'Woh kya soch rahe honge?' ('What would the person be thinking?')

Lesson:
It is just as important to ask 'What would they be thinking?' as it is to ask 'How am I feeling?'

Papa struggled his entire professional life. His risks didn't pay off, we were perpetually in debt, and went through some extremely tough times financially.

But one thing that never changed was how hard he continued to work.
I was always amazed. Always wondered what kept him going.

Lesson:
Nothing matters more in life than showing up every day.
To work, to assume responsibilities, to nurture relationships.

Whenever I won any award or did anything praise-worthy, Ma would of course be happy, but she would instantly shower her favourite blessing

'Bhagwaan tumhe humesha zameen par rakhe.'
('May god always keep you grounded.')

Lesson:
Never forget where you have come from.

Be it a family gathering, a wedding ceremony or even a normal dinner, Papa will always carry his book of Kashmiri songs.

In the hope that someone asks him to sing.
He believes he sings well (and he does).
So he can't fathom why people won't ask him to sing :)

Lesson:
If you do not believe in yourself, no one else will.

I dropped out of my PhD and came back to India. At 24, I had no plans, no goals, no direction, no money. Ma and Papa weren't too happy, but to their credit they did their best to hide their anguish.

One day, I still remember I was brushing my teeth when Ma came to me and sheepishly said,

'Would you want to consider taking the IAS examination? You know, because I think you might make a good IAS officer'

It was a request.
For me to consider something.
I politely declined, but realized how blessed I was to have parents who would 'request' their kids to consider.

Lesson:
Respect doesn't come from title, age or experience.
It comes from conduct.

I have lost count of the times Papa would step into a situation whenever everything else had failed and redeem the moment.

Be it as trivial as 'wedding guests have arrived and the food isn't even prepared' to as critical as 'where will we arrange money for his ticket to the US?'

Lesson:
Whenever everyone else fails you, you still have yourself.

Ma has always stood for perfection. But she has a very interesting and inspiring definition of it.

Perfection is when you do something with such finesse that people are left amazed at how you even did it.

But for you, it is not a big deal.
It is a habit.
It is natural.

Lesson:
Perfection is personal.
It is what makes others wonder.
But for you it is the only way you know!

Both Ma and Papa come from Srinagar, where they grew up with little privilege.
They did not go to any top school.
They did not have any stamp that would set them for life.

They just worked their way through. Like most others of their generation.

And it often makes me cry to realize how much they went through just to ensure that my sister and I got the best we could.

We went to good schools, we were given the freedom to live our lives, we were always loved and taken care of.
And I am convinced that much of what we are today is because of the upbringing we had.

We lived a life without money, in extreme conditions quite often, but we always made sure we had a good time.

Four of us on our Bajaj scooter, going to India Gate with a bag containing a pressure cooker full of peas pulao, a sheet to sit on, plates and cutlery.
And ending the evening with the 5-rupee ice candy from Kwality.

I guess this is where I got the courage to pursue happiness.
I knew what it was to live without money.

But I didn't know what it was to live without happiness.

Today, one of my key goals is to give my parents all the money they need.
To do whatever they want.

They already know what it is to be happy :)

Letters to our kids that I never wrote but should have . . .

Dear Vidur

Each time you cry watching a cartoon, because of what you think is something unfair, I hope and pray that you never forget how you felt. I hope your definition of what is unfair, remains just as pure.

Love

Dear Uzma

I didn't think we needed you. I was worried whether you would turn out to be a boy (two boys – no no!). I was worried I wouldn't have the time for you.

But I am so glad you came to our world.

You complete me.

Love

Dear Vidur

Recall how badly you wanted a bicycle when you were five and we couldn't afford it. We somehow managed. When you saw it, you broke down.
So when we asked you, 'What's the best gift you've got from us?', we expected you to say that cycle.

You said, 'Uzma.'

You are so precious!

Love

Dear Uzma

Every time you stand in front of the mirror and sing and dance like you don't care, you remind me how wonderful life is.

Confession.

I do the same now, in front of the mirror.

Love

Dear Vidur

We were forcing you to sleep, when all you
wanted to do was stand in front of the window
and feel the rain drops fall on you.
So you pretended to sleep.

And when we left, you went to the window
and felt the rain drops on you.
You did the right thing.

Love

Dear Uzma

Your name in Urdu means the greatest.
No pressure! :)

Love

Dear Vidur

Your name in Hindi means the intelligent or
wise one.
No pressure! :)

Love

Dear Uzma

The big highlight of the day for you is choosing the clothes you will wear. You devote your heart, mind and soul to it, as if your life depends on it. And once it's done you always feel proud that you did it.

Live this way. Forever!

Love

Dear Vidur

I love how excited you get when we get Amazon packages. That is yet another cardboard box for you to play with. Make robots, kitchen sets, gaming arcades.

You see things.
And I hope and pray you continue to, forever.

Love

Dear Uzma

The best part of the day is when we wind up your toys together.

You look forward to it. Cleaning the mess. Sorting the chaos. Putting things back. Before you put on your 'suit-night'.

Continue doing this forever. It is your mess. You fix it. Feel happy doing so.

Love

Dear Vidur

You love irritating Uzma. You scare her, shout at her, scold her. Even hit her.

But then you say sorry. You cry if she cries. You read books to her to console her.

You have a gift to see when people like what you do and when they don't.

Don't change that.

Love

Dear Uzma

You express yourself as if you are an adult. What you like, what you don't. What you want

and what you don't. What makes you happy
and what doesn't.

You seem to know yourself very well.

That is a gift. Always work on that.

Love

Dear Vidur

The world will continue to impose its definition
of success and failure on you. We are guilty of
it too.

Go ahead and define success and failure the
way you want to.

Live your own life.
Not someone else's.

Love

Dear Uzma

The world will continue to impose its definition
of success and failure on you. We are guilty of
it too.

Go ahead and define success and failure the way you want to.

Live your own life.
Not someone else's.

Love

Dear Vidur

Every time you ask me to share our money/ice cream/biscuits with the kids on the street because they do not have what we have, you remind me of how all of us were, before we became who we are.

Please don't become who we are.

Love

Dear Uzma

When you read books to yourself, despite the fact that you can't read, you still enjoy the book just as much as you would if we were to read it out to you.

Sometimes even more.

It is the story in your head that is the most important story. Always remember that.

Love

Dear Vidur

You once wanted to become a soldier. Then a watchman. Then a robot. Then an artist.

You know what? I really wish you become ALL of that and more. Why become only one thing in our life? We have only one!

Love

Dear Uzma

You call Vidur, Dada. It means brother in Bengali and grandfather in Hindi.

But you don't know that yet.
When you do, don't change it because it doesn't sound right. Keep it, because that is where you have come from.

Don't ever forget where you have come from.

Love

Dear Vidur

Mumma and I grew up with virtually no money.

But you go to an air-conditioned school.
Our job then is to constantly remind you of
your privilege.

You haven't earned this.
You were gifted this.

Don't ever be proud of it. Be grateful for it.

Love

Dear Uzma

There is something special about how you
sing along with Alexa, each time Dada plays
your favourite song.

You pretend you are a rockstar.

Tell you what?

You are!
You are whoever you think you are.

Love

Dear Vidur

Your kindness, your respectful nature, your cheerful demeanor and your ability to immerse yourself into anything is precious.

You make us so proud of you, meri jaan.

Don't change!

Love

Dear Uzma

Your energy, your antics, your cheerfulness brings so much happiness to our lives. I didn't think we could experience love from a child like you have made us feel.

You make us so happy, meri jaan.

Always be happy.

Love

EPILOGUE

've had multiple failures in my life. I talk about them often. You've read about a lot of them in this book.

However, right now, I want to talk to you about a bit that isn't a failure: my relationship with time.

Ever since I was a child, I remember measuring my time.

I used to track meticulously what I did in a day, hour-wise, in a notebook while at school, then moved to Excel and today I use apps.

Till date, time is the one thing I guard ferociously.

Everything in my life is on my calendar.

My workouts.

My video shoots.

Birthdays and anniversaries.

Bills to pay, insurance renewal reminders.

I even schedule my free time.

Most people think it is imprisoning. For me, it's liberating.

Because it allows me to be more of who I am.

But, why am I talking about this at the end of the book?

Because no matter how many failures you've had, no matter how many heartburns you've been through, or how many unexpected storms you have withered – there is always a part of you that serves as a tent pole that comes to help you in every area of your life.

For me, it is my relationship with time.

All the things I schedule are things I prioritize in my life.

I do them repeatedly, clinically, because I have promised myself to do so.

And over time, they have become habits.

Habits that have taken me out of my biggest failures and generated opportunities I could not have imagined for myself.

While this entire book was about guiding

you to make choices from a point of awareness and not ignorance, there is one last thing I want to take you towards: that no one except you will be aware of.

What is your superpower?

Time is mine.

What's yours?

When I talk about it, I'm not talking about following your passion or finding the career of your choice.

But one thing that always keeps you going when nothing seems to be going right.

It could be your relentless discipline.

It could be your dedication and commitment.

Could be your simple approach towards life.

Could even be your attention to detail.

Could be your friendly demeanour.

Or your athleticism.

Or even your rebellious nature that has worked wonders for you.

You have that superpower already.

As you go out into the world and do your own epic shit, I suggest you take this armour with you. And you shall never return home defeated.

Because, the powerful things that lie within us are often the easiest to overlook.

ankur warikoo, signing off!

ACKNOWLEDGEMENTS

This book is a terrific example of borrowed thoughts and inspiration. None of what I have shared with you would have been possible if it wasn't for several people who have helped me with their worldviews, their motivation and their kind words.

I will start with Chiki, who as early as 2014 met me for the first time and said, 'You have a lot of books in you.' She saw an author in me long before I could ever see one in myself. Thank you for your belief, Chiki.

To the Juggernaut team, who were patient with my endless edits.

Nishtha, who leads content for wariCrew and is frankly the reason this book even exists. She went through years of content, collated what she felt was powerful and then weaved it all together.

The entire wariCrew, who make me so proud of what we are doing and how we are going about it. You all make me fly!

Cecilia Ma'am, my class teacher from high school, who showed me that a good teacher can change a life forever.

Kunal, Mukesh, Mishra for making school something I will always cherish and would never want to forget.

Sameer, Modi, Gusty, Nishant, Korde, Vineet – who made my stay in the US memorable. Those two years shaped me up in a way like nothing else did and you were a big part of it.

The ISB Batch of 2006 – you all continue to inspire me. It is fascinating how each one in the batch has wonderfully chosen their own definition of success over the year, through which they help others define theirs.

Akshat, Anshuman, Shintu – my colleagues at Kearney, who taught me when I knew nothing, were patient when I fumbled and continue to be friends who encourage.

Pahwa, for giving me my first entrepreneurial break. I will forever be grateful for that opportunity.

Oli, for teaching me about entrepreneurship in a year that I couldn't have experienced even in a decade.

Mohit, for believing in us when no one else believed in us. And supporting us, when no one was ready to.

Everyone who worked at Groupon and nearbuy – those nine years shaped me as a leader, as an operator and as a person. I will forever be grateful and I fondly remember what a lovely institution you helped me shape.

Ravi and Snehesh for being the best cofounders I could have asked for. For believing in me, despite my inadequacies and calling my bullshit when needed.

Banno, Supriya, PK, Mitu, Shipra, Anoop, Rohit, Apoorva, Kamal, Shyamala, Meera, Venky for being such wonderful friends.

Bubbs, Singla, Bali, Chishti for being the friends that I need in life. You never let me take myself seriously, you help me, advise me and continue to entertain my poor jokes!

Radhika, for being a sister I had so much fun growing up with. To see her do so well and follow her dreams – it feels like she is my best student:)

Ruchi's entire family for being so welcoming of me; Gautam for wonderfully becoming part of our family.

Ma and Papa, for teaching me the values that form the foundation of everything that I know. You have been unbelievably patient and supportive of my rather crazy decisions in life and I hope to be that parent to Vidur and Uzma.

Vidur and Uzma, for adding meaning to my life in a way I could never have imagined. I live for you.

And finally, Ruchi, without whom I am no body. We have been together for 21 years now. We have practically grown up together.

I know a large part of who I am is because you always saw the best in me. Thank you for being in my life. I love you.

ANKUR'S NEXT BOOK

The year 2020 was when I started working on *DO EPIC SHIT*. Originally it was planned as a memoir, a narration of my life experiences. The more I sat down with my stories, the more I realized that it was too soon to share them. I was still 40 and while that may seem really old to most of you, I cannot even begin to tell you how young 40 feels.

So at some point in 2021, I moved to a different theme.

I asked myself an honest question, *'Who do I want to write the book for?'*

By this time, I was already creating content across all platforms and was witnessing a reception I hadn't imagined.

The more I created content, the more I seemed to be attracting a young crowd that was resonating with it.

And as I continued to ask the question *'Who do I want to write the book for?'*, the answer became obvious.

I wanted to write it for you.

You are either in your late teens or your 20s.

You could be in your 30s and 40s as well, or even beyond that, but that is you just being gracious :)

You think you are already late in life.

You had planned so much, but quite often you feel you have let yourself and others down.

You think everyone around you is so sorted, and you are the only loser who hasn't figured out life.

You want help, but you do not know whom to ask, what to ask, how to ask.

I wanted *DO EPIC SHIT* to be for you.

To comfort you by saying that we all fail.

To convince you that you are not late.

To impress upon you that life is simple. Not easy. Simple!

I wanted *DO EPIC SHIT* to become your go-to book whenever you are low.

When you do not know who could help, if at all.

And it humbles me how so many of you have helped me achieve this.

Not a day passes without me getting a DM or a message from a reader about how this book is the first book they have finished.

How this book is the first book they have read.

How that page, that they had randomly opened, was exactly what they had needed to hear that day.

DO EPIC SHIT was my step to get you to think.

To reflect. To ponder.

And to make it easy for you to do so.

And for my next book, I want to take the next step.

My next book, whose name I shall not share with you yet, will be a guide for you.

If *DO EPIC SHIT* provoked you and got you thinking, my second book will attempt to offer a way to solve your problems.

Problems that you and I encounter every day.

How to take tough decisions

How to build a habit of reading

How to pick the right career

How to deal with failure

How to make money work for you

How to have a good relationship with parents

How to say no

How to build good habits

50+ life questions, answered in a format that will be easy to read, easy to comprehend and easy to implement.

I am so excited to be writing this book for you. A book that I know I would have benefited from immensely in my early years as an adult.

And I am convinced you will find it remarkable, too.

It will serve as a quick guide whenever you are stuck.

Turn to the page of your current situation, and the next few pages will hopefully give you a way out of the situation.

The book hits stands in December 2022.
Stay tuned.
Until then, keep doing epic shit. :)

A NOTE ON THE AUTHOR

Ankur Warikoo is an entrepreneur, teacher, content creator and mentor. Ankur founded nearbuy.com and was its CEO from its inception in 2015 until 2019. Prior to that, Ankur was the founding CEO of Groupon's India business. Today he spends his time creating content, teaching online and mentoring first-time founders.

To download the app scan the QR Code
with a QR scanner app

For our complete catalogue, visit www.juggernaut.in
To submit your book, send a synopsis and two
sample chapters to books@juggernaut.in
For all other queries, write to contact@juggernaut.in